PASSION FOR GOLF

PASSION FOR GOLF

IN PURSUIT OF THE
INNERMOST GAME

ROLAND MERULLO

THE LYONS PRESS

Designed by Compset, Inc.

Printed in the United States of America

10 9 8 7 6 5 4 3 2 1

Library of Congress Cataloging-in-Publication Data

Merullo, Roland.
    Passion for golf: in pursuit of the innermost game / Roland Merullo.
        p. cm.
    ISBN 1-58574-162-0
    1. Golf—Psychological aspects. 2. Golfers—Conduct of life. 3. Merullo, Roland. I.
Title.

GV979.P75 M47 2000
796.352'01'9 21; aa05 07-21—dc00

00-59914

For Eileen Merullo

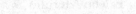

Misled by fancy's meteor ray
By passion driven
But yet the light that led astray
Was light from heaven

—Robert Burns, "The Vision"

CONTENTS

ACKNOWLEDGMENTS

My heartfelt thanks to Nick Lyons for his expert guidance and inspiration, to Craig Nova for suggesting this book, and to Amanda for encouraging my passion for the game.

PREFACE

Something like fifty million people in the world play golf. Probably a third of them are, like me, passionately in love with the game. Week after week and season after season we can be found on our manicured pastures, knocking a dimpled white ball in the general direction of a small hole in the earth. We scribble on colorful cards with undersized pencils, we toss handfuls of grass clippings into the air and watch where the wind takes them, we ride in funny white carts, or we carry or tow a cylindrical bag filled with a peculiar assortment of implements. And before we actually swing one of these implements at the dimpled ball, we engage in what might seem to the alien eye like a highly evolved mating dance: raising and lowering our head, shifting our feet, flexing our knees and wagging our arms, twitching our rear end like a pigeon coaxing a reluctant love partner.

Comical as it may seem to the outside observer, golf is a magical feast once you are actually playing. It soothes, challenges, frustrates, delights—as does any love. This short book is an exploration of that love, and it circles around the idea that golf offers a thousand lessons about living: lessons that can be applied to marriage and child rearing, friendship, business, and, mostly, lessons that point us toward a state of inner steadiness and peace.

In considering the possibility of this peace, I have made use of the words of the mystics, a term that is meant here in its widest sense. To me, a mystic is anyone who looks at life through a broad lens, seeking ways of connecting rather than dividing, and starting from the assumption that we are built to be happy and calm most of the time despite the sea of pain and disappointment in which we all swim. To the mystic, everything is part of the watery web of life. Touch one fiber of it—family, work, golf—and the reverberations are felt in the farthest corners. Most serious golfers have an intuitive understanding of this connectedness. Most of us can see the anxiety or peace of our off-course lives reflected in our game. And we suspect it works in the other direction as well: Playing golf in a devoted way, we learn something about ourselves, and carry that knowledge back into more important arenas.

1
THE OTHER EIGHTY PERCENT

Golf is twenty percent mechanics and technique. The other eighty percent is philosophy, humor, tragedy, romance, melodrama, companionship, camaraderie, cussedness and conversation.

—Grantland Rice, noted American
sportswriter and avid golfer

I play at the Worthington Golf Club, a nine-hole course that sits high up in the foothills of the Berkshire Mountains in western Massachusetts. Like many courses, Worthington offers several different leagues for its members to join—men's, women's, mixed. These are important parts of the social life of the club, and give ordinary players a chance to enjoy the heat of competition.

On a Thursday evening last summer the men's league matches were canceled because of persistent heavy rain. My partner and I had teed off in the first foursome of the afternoon—at that point the weather was bad but uncertainly so—and we didn't realize the matches had been called off until all four of us had putted out on the first green. That hole is a short, straight par four—333 yards from the white tees, 351 from the blues—and from where we stood we could look back toward the clubhouse and see the other league members walking away from the tee area and the pro shop and getting into their cars. The rain was falling steadily by then, moderately hard, but the afternoon was mild. Our opponents put covers over their clubs, zipped up their rain slickers, and headed back down the fairway toward home. But Jeff and I lingered on the apron, studying the clouds, the movement of the trees, the small puddles gathering in the two tough bunkers right and left. After a minute I said, "Let's keep going."

"I'm game," he answered. We walked over to the second tee.

The second, third, and fourth holes at Worthington are all short but challenging par fours that spread along the steep, east-facing slope of the course. From the second tee you walk straight downhill (I once saw a friend's self-propelled cart take off down this slope and nearly get away from him) past a view of farmland and distant hillsides to a small, capricious, convex green. The green was shedding water beautifully that day—the one thing I like about it. When we finished the hole I believe we both stood at even par, a slightly better-than-average start for us. From there it would have been a long uphill walk to the clubhouse. Though small lakes were forming in the low spots on the cart track, and cool breaths of wind were pushing sheets of rain across the next tee, we saw no reason to turn back.

The third hole is flatter and more difficult, a 110-degree dogleg right with a bunker strategically placed at the outside part of the knee joint and a 140- to 210-yard second shot, depending on how close you manage to cut the corner with your first. The green is unprotected by traps or water hazards, but there is thick rough to the left and behind, and a steep drop-off to the right.

Our games faltered a bit there. The clouds tumbled and spun in a gray and purple circus but showed no signs of thinning, and the rain began to take on that hard, steady aspect that signals it's settling in for the long haul. We followed all the usual bad-weather precautions: took off our gloves between shots and folded them into our jacket pock-

5

ets, balanced the umbrellas over our bags while we putted. But as Lao-tzu said:

Under heaven nothing is more soft and yielding than
  water
Yet for attacking the solid and strong, nothing is better;
It has no equal.

We began to get really wet.

The fourth hole bends back up along the side of the hill, its fairway growing narrower and more tilted as it goes, as if to punish the stronger driver. From the green you are usually treated to the fifteen-mile eastward view again, but the clouds were closing down over those rolling hills, the rain drawing a gray curtain toward us. It's a contrary, troublesome putting surface on the best of days; the ball actually runs uphill from certain angles. (As veteran Worthington golfers will tell you if you're playing our greens for the first time: "Everything breaks toward the potato fields"—east of the course.) We managed it fairly well, considering.

By the time we stood on the fifth tee our bags and grips were thoroughly wet, our pants soaked from the knee down, the brims of our hats and the sleeves of our rain jackets and the tines of our umbrellas dripping out a Morse code that seemed to be counseling surrender. It's a difficult hole, too: a 201-yard par three with what is reputed to be the smallest green in Massachusetts. The green is guarded by a deep bunker to the front left and, close in on the other sides, a species of rough that is worthy, on a good day, of Walt Whitman's description of grass: "the beautiful uncut hair of graves."

There was nothing especially beautiful about it on that afternoon. To make things more problematic, the clubhouse comes into view again at that point—in fact, it's only a three-minute walk from the fifth green—and then on holes six and seven and the beginning of eight you move away and lose sight of it. So that would have been the moment to pack it in and head home. But one of us must have made a long putt; or perhaps the rain eased up for a few seconds, or we spotted another player on the first fairway and were ashamed to quit. Whatever the reason, we finished the fifth and teed up again on the sixth without debate.

The sixth is another par three—148 yards that run so steeply downhill, many league members hit only a wedge. The green is two-tiered, guarded all across the front by a pair of high-lipped, ten-foot bunkers, and above, to left and right, by the spreading branches of two tall maple trees. Worthington's course superintendent—who is also the club champion and holder of the course record—sometimes likes to cut the cup only a foot or so above the point where the bottom tier drops away. By then, however, the ease or difficulty of the pin placement didn't matter much to us. As is sometimes the case when you drive along a highway at night in snow or thick fog, we were forced to narrow down our range of attention to the matter at hand and nothing else. Just to make some kind of solid contact with the ball, we had to stop worrying about the rain, stop feeling the trickle of water running down inside our collars, stop caring about the score.

On the seventh, what might be called Worthington's signature hole—a 528-yard par five with a tilted fairway, a brook, two difficult bunkers, and a steeply pitched green—my game began to pull apart at its wet seams. Soggy, meaty divots flopped after my iron shots like so many unhappy mongrels chasing a fleeing master. If memory serves, it took me three shots to reach the pine tree that pinches the fairway only two hundred yards out from the tee, and eight more strokes before I fished my ball out of the two inches of standing water at the bottom of the cup. I had a moment then, just the smallest moment, of wondering what we were doing out there in that weather.

The eighth is another par-five, ninety-degree dogleg left. The first leg is 175 yards uphill, and the second runs along a tilted 300 yards to another multilevel green. At seventeen hundred feet above sea level, it's the highest hole in the state. We were sloshing along through standing water by then, a black sky scudding in circles overhead. The clubhouse appeared again, its warm-looking white bulk gazing out over an empty parking lot. After you finish putting on the eighth, you have to walk away from the clubhouse fifty yards to reach the ninth tee, and we did; at that point it seemed absurd not to finish.

The ninth is one of the easier holes on the course, a simple par three that, somehow, doesn't end up getting parred or birdied as often as it should. A boulder beside the tee bears a plaque commemorating a day in 1972 when two members—one seventy-six years old, the other seventy-one—playing in the same foursome had back-to-back holes-in-one. Jeff and I had no such hopes. A fresh wind had come up out of the north. We could hear the rain hitting against the leaves of the trees, and we felt as if we were playing in a medium of water and water, not land and air.

Chilled to the bone, we finished the hole and changed into dry socks and shoes. Afterward, I distinctly remember sitting at a table in the clubhouse with Jeff and his wife, Lisa, eating dinner, drinking hot tea, and looking out at the practice green. The reason I remember it so well is that it seemed to me the drumming on the windows had grown a notch quieter, and I found myself wondering if maybe I should just step back out there in the drizzle for a little more work on my short game before full dark set in. I realized then what my real relationship was to the game of golf.

2
THE SWEETNESS OF DOING NOTHING

*I simply wanted to do nothing. . . . My nothing
meant simply to play golf. . . . This may seem
incredible to those who have never fallen hopelessly
in love with the game; but I can see the charm and
temptation even now; for golf or any other pastime
can be much more than a mere hitting of the ball; it
can be, however poor a one, a life to be lived.*

—Bernard Darwin, member
of the 1922 British Walker Cup team

Though golf is sometimes considered an activity for comfort seekers and lazy millionaires, the story in the first chapter is a typical one in golfing circles. Those of us who are devoted to the game play in the rain and heat and snow and fog, in gale-force winds, in swarms of mosquitoes and blackflies, in the first and last minutes of daylight, when we're suffering from a cold or pulled muscles, when we haven't slept the night before, when there are other things we should be doing: cleaning out our rain gutters or spending an extra few hours preparing for Monday's presentation. And when we're not playing, we spend a good amount of time thinking about playing. We putt on the living room carpet. We stare at the Golf Channel and read golf magazines in the cold heart of winter, we gaze mournfully out at the drifting snow and count the weeks until spring. We move south if we can, or at least take vacations in the sun and carry our clubs along. We practice our backswing in empty elevators. We can remember shots we hit a decade ago, sometimes even replaying whole matches, stroke by stroke and putt by putt, in our mind.

How strange, this passion for an activity that, from the outside, must seem so absurd. What can account for it? What is it about golf that turns otherwise sane, reasonable men and women into people who will happily spend an hour at a cocktail party talking about different types of wedges? No doubt some of the attraction has to do with being outdoors in the sun and air, in the weather. Some of it is about being with friends, or getting a little exercise, or slipping free, for a few hours, from the thousand nagging responsibilities of modern life. But our affection has a deeper and more mysterious quality to it as well: Golf is a game and more than a game. Playing a round—on any course, at any level of ability—is a condensed version of living a life: There are triumphs and disasters, overall goals and interme-

16

diate ones, bits of unexpected luck both good and bad. While the trip can be made in the company of others, there is something inherently solitary about it; and our mistakes can usually be compensated for, but they always count. The golf course is a kind of training ground where we practice being human, where we nourish ourselves from a well of satisfaction and do battle with mock-ups of more dangerous off-course demons. Down deep, every devoted golfer understands this link between golf and life, this hidden purpose of the game. It's part of what keeps us out there in the rain.

To begin with, there is—on the first tee especially, but at other moments, too—that same sense of youthful hope and possibility we feel when we embark on a new relationship, or a new job, or move to a new place. To paraphrase Walt Whitman, we expect the best from ourselves, and from life. But why? In a world so full of trouble, of individual histories flecked with pain, what is the root of this optimism?

Usually, when we begin a new stage of life, we know the realities—the psychological obstacles to enduring love, if it's a new relationship; the potential for a difficult boss or arrogant coworkers at the new job; the fickle weather or unpleasant neighbor in our new town—just as we know we will encounter some trouble during our round: pulled putts, errant approach shots, bad lies. But on that first tee we somehow convince ourselves to set these realities aside. We have to. No one begins a round thinking he will shoot his worst score, just as no one gets married thinking she will be miserable. Without a certain amount of hope, perhaps even a measure of false hope, we would not put the tee in the ground, the ring on the finger, our signature on the deed.

But then the round begins, life moves forward, and shot by shot, day by day, we trade a wisp of fantasy for a block of reality. Our perfect mate shows an imperfection or two; our adorable baby grows up and begins to make demands. Our booming first tee shot has a tail on it, kicks six or eight yards to the right, and leaves us with a sidehill lie in bristly rough at the edge of the trees. What we do at this point reveals a great deal about who we are. Perhaps we curse the course architect, or the architect of life. Or maybe, as the Tibetan

Buddhist teacher Chogyam Trungpa put it, we "drive all blames into one"—that is, take the responsibility for the situation onto our own shoulders, whether the situation is fair or not, whether we believe we deserve it or not. Maybe it begins to occur to us then that at least some of our troubles can be traced to our own faults: that our mate is so talkative because we are so reserved, that our tee shot kicked right because we got our elbow out away from us on the downswing. What do we do then? Complain more convincingly? Swing the same way, only harder? Buy a new set of clubs?

Golf is just a game, just fun. But anyone who plays it seriously knows that devotion to the game automatically shows us things about ourselves, some of which we like, some of which we'd rather not see. The same is true of any serious commitment—living or working with another person for a long time, raising children, sticking with a career, building a business, pursuing one kind of spiritual path or another. The hardships and the pleasures are like bottles knocking up against our boat, with little notes inside on which are scribbled helpful suggestions.

What we do with this information is an individual matter: Staying married or staying at a job is not always a prescription for wisdom, just as loving golf is no automatic cure for our ills and bad habits. As living proof of this, there are a fair number of people who play often, and even play well, yet remain the obnoxious, boorish, petty egomaniacs they were before they ever picked up a club. You see them—or, more accurately, hear them—on courses everywhere. Loud, inconsiderate, bereft of honor, they seem, simply by the force of their own narcissism, able to spoil the weather over a fairway or the atmosphere in a clubhouse. They are constitutionally incapable of fixing a ballmark on a green.

But I'm not thinking of those people when I say "passionate golfer," or "devoted golfer," or "serious golfer." By those words I mean people who truly love the game, and true love—marital, parental, even love for one's work—has both an assertive and a humble aspect to it. Serious golfers know that, in golf as in life, they have taken on a partner they will never conquer. In fact, though, love isn't about conquering. It's about a kind of full engagement, a willingness to stay connected when everything works and when nothing does, when every putt drops and when none of them do. The devoted golfer might shove his bag angrily into his locker or the trunk of his car after an ugly round, but he'll come back the next day or the next week fueled by fresh hope. The devoted husband, wife, or parent suffers through periods of estrangement and disappointment but returns to the field of love expecting something better, hoping for—almost demanding from life—some reawakened sweetness. It is devotion, not perfection, that teaches.

Teresa of Avila—the fifteenth-century Spanish nun, so revered by Catholic contemplatives—came up with the idea of likening our spiritual predicament to an "interior castle," an imaginary structure composed of seven "rooms," arranged concentrically. The outermost room represents the first serious stirring of spiritual feeling, the first sense that there might be something more to life than just a doomed, eighty-year stretch spent fleeing pain and chasing pleasure. And her innermost room corresponds to an ecstatic union with the

Divine, a Zen enlightenment, a sort of walking-around god-liness.

Sometimes I look at golf that way—the innermost room being a place where we are perfectly aligned with both the joys and miseries of our game, at peace with ourselves on the course, grateful, satisfied, while at the same time working to improve. Some golfers would rather not think so deeply about it. They are content to go out every day or every other Saturday and focus on lowering their score, or just enjoy a cigar or a couple of beers and whack the ball around with friends. More power to them; the game has room for all kinds of attitudes. For others, though—for the contemplative golfer, the devotee, there is a moment when he or she enters that outermost room and is drawn into golf at a deeper level. Hazrat Inayat Khan, a Sufi mystic, said about the initiation into the spiritual life that at such a time, "a person feels he has suddenly awakened to quite another world."

In golf this awakening means you start to pay a heightened attention—to your mental state, your grip, your posture, the feel of the clubhead, the rules, the course design, perhaps the words of famous players and instructors. Instead of locking golf away in a separate box marked PLEASURE, you begin to believe that the person you are on the course teaches you about the person you are off the course. You begin, as a husband or wife does after the first few happy months and the first serious arguments, to enter into a deeper level of communion with the object of your affection.

At this point, in marriage and in golf, a certain amount of humility is helpful—a measure of introspection. You have to step into the safely closed-up inner vault that contains your surest defenses, and reexamine them. You have to begin to admit what a terrible, what an atrocious, what an embarrassingly bad putter you are, or how seldom you actually look at your wife when you are talking to her. You have to begin the hard work of changing old habits. As compensation for this work and this new degree of attention, marriage offers its quiet, profound joys, and the game of golf reveals its secrets, room by room, year by year.

Along the way we will likely become better players. But I think the urge to improve, the dream of becoming a scratch golfer or a winner on the PGA tour, satisfying as those accomplishments would be, is only a part of our obsession. The other part has something to do with that innermost room, with the promise of a deeper, calmer pleasure.

"There is a wine which the mystic drinks," Hazrat Khan said, "and that wine is ecstasy." We are served small portions of this ecstasy every time we play: we sink a crooked downhill putt that we've missed a dozen times in the past; we birdie our home course's toughest hole; or we just give an extra moment of attention to the darker and lighter bands of grass on a newly mowed fairway. In any relationship with a friend or beloved, in the course of raising a child or devoting ourselves to a career, there are moments like this as well: The pure blaze of early love is rekindled, the happy idealism of the first days of our child's life returns to us, and the failures of the past—its triple bogeys, three-putts, and painful estrangements—are forgotten. Over the long run it cannot be a dream of perfection that's really urging us on—who expects eighteen holes-in-one? Who expects, or even wants, a child or a spouse who pleases us with every word and decision?—it's the hope of being, someday, at peace with the imperfection. This rugged equanimity is the prerequisite for the ecstasy all mystics speak of; not the innermost room, perhaps, but surely a corridor leading there.

These intimations of a calmer state, a higher joy, are part of the great gift golf offers, the secret jewels that crown our mad affection for it. *Quies,* the Desert Fathers (those great sand players of the fourth-century Arabian desert) called it. *Shalom,* in early Hebrew texts. Peace, rest, a kind of quiet spiritual abundance. Not putting-our-feet-up-on-the-Barcalounger-with-a-beer kind of rest, not giving-up-on-everything kind of peace, but interior rest. Golf points us in that direction.

Thomas Merton said of the Desert Fathers: "The 'rest' which these men sought was simply the sanity and poise of a being that no longer has to look at itself because it is carried away by the perfection of freedom that is in it." He didn't say "perfection," but "perfection of freedom"—the radical idea that, while we can't choose what happens to us, we have the freedom to choose our response to it.

Once golf draws us in, once we get to the place where we are willing to walk around in the rain for a couple of hours or hit two hundred balls at the driving range, then, for all our peculiar antics in all kinds of weather, we gain in sanity and poise; we almost can't help it. It's as if we have been fitted with a new set of eyes. Instead of cursing the course, we look at our swing, our dread of failure or subtle fear of success, our stubbornness and anger and ego. There can be rough edges to the process. We can start to envy the careless hacker or the arrogant pro, just as the married woman can have moments of envying her single counterpart, or the father of a teenager his childless pal. But little by little the rough edges get worn away, the gusts of temper settle. Not everyone becomes a great golfer, just as not everyone achieves his dream life or raises grateful and loving kids. But that kind of success is not what the innermost room is all about. That's not the real goal of golf, or of living.

26

3
THE MANY
FACES OF EGO

The ego and its grasping are at the root of all our suffering.

—Sogyal Rinpoche, Tibetan Buddhist master,
The Tibetan Book of Living and Dying

I believe that is true. I believe it's also true that the ego and its grasping are what stand between us and a more deeply pleasing experience on the golf course.

Before I joined Worthington, I used to play in the men's league at a course called Edge Hill in Ashfield, Massachusetts. Only a year or so before I started playing there, Edge Hill had been cut out of farmland and forest. It is hill country, and the course's architect and owner, Mark Graves, laid out his nine holes in such a way that the steep terrain figures prominently on certain holes but does not come into play at all on others. As a result, his course offers a certain kind of golf challenge more typical of New England than of most other parts of the country: flat, straightforward stretches that alternate with severe slopes; steeply elevated greens, blind tee shots, dense woods to either side of the fairway, and tilted landing areas that exact a stiff penalty for all but the most accurately placed shots.

I played in the Tuesday-night men's league, and my partner there was a sandy-haired Vietnam veteran named Walt. Walt was five foot seven or eight, with a powerful build and a real devotion to the game. He had a single-digit handicap and a tight, smooth swing, but, strong as he was, he wasn't a distance hitter off the tee. I had a handicap somewhere in the high twenties at the start of that season— a bit lower by the end—but if I did manage to make solid contact, I almost always outdrove him, sometimes by twenty yards or more. Some rounds I outdistanced him on every driving hole, but not once all summer did I finish the day with a lower score. I wasn't wise enough then to see that Walt had been put into my life by the golfing gods to teach me about the destructive nature of my own ego.

The first hole at Edge Hill is a complicated and beautiful par five, a perfect trap for the egotistical golfer. From an elevated tee you look down on what, a few years before, had been grazing land. Once you reach the bottom of the hill on which the tees are set and cross a steeply banked stream, the fairway gradually flattens and spreads. At one point it must be a hundred yards wide. The stream curls back across it there, angling right to left away from the hole at a distance of between two hundred and three hundred yards, so that you have a choice of taking a long or medium iron and aiming for the right side of that hundred-yard-wide target, or hitting a driver or three-wood and aiming farther left. It's trickier than that, though, because the first option might leave you behind the large tree that has been left there just to make the short route to the hole less appealing. And even if you manage to place your tee shot carefully away from the tree, you still face a second shot that requires a difficult carry over deep rough and the meandering stream.

Most people aim left, at a wide, flat landing area that leaves a longer but safer angle of approach to an undulating green. Par five, four hundred and ninety yards from the middle tees.

In my first league match, my first year of playing regularly again after back surgery, I had the bad fortune to hit

31

what was probably my best drive of the season off that first tee. I then had the even worse luck of following my drive with as close as I have ever come to a perfect three-wood shot: a high, 230-yard fade that landed softly, rolled a little way, and came to a stop eight feet past the pin. I had a curving downhill putt for eagle, which I left short by three inches, but I was happy enough to take the birdie.

The bad fortune came from the fact that my head was so swollen by reaching the green in two that, for the rest of the year, I never tried to do anything *but* reach it in two, and never again made better than par.

Golf is unique among all sports in the degree to which it teases the ego. On any given afternoon a lucky twenty-eight-handicapper can make a shot, even play a hole, as well as the best PGA pro. He might use a seven-iron from the same place the pro uses a wedge, but on that blessed day there will be a slight click when the metal makes contact with the ball, and the ball will leap off the clubface and sail along in a magnificent trajectory, seem to hang for a moment at the top of its arc as if expecting applause from the angels, then drop gracefully back to earth, slap onto the green, and roll to within a foot of the pin.

Could that ever happen in, say, hockey? Even once, never mind two or three times in a season? Could the forty-year-old, once-a-week left-winger *ever* smack a one-timer from the blue line into the top corner with Dominik Hasek in the net? Could he step up to the plate and line a Pedro Martinez fastball off the wall in left? Have a good day and sprint the hundred meters in 9.5 seconds?

In golf parlance a shot like that three-wood is what "keeps you coming back." (A European pro I once played with called it a "see you tomorrow.") It rings in your memory for the rest of the week like a lover's voice whispering endearments. Part of the unique joy and beauty of the game comes from the fact that anyone, on any given afternoon, can make a great shot like that, or hole a forty-foot putt. One of my cousins scored a hole-in-one the first time she ever played, on her first swing. (The other people in her foursome were hugging her and clapping and shouting and she wondered what the big fuss was about: The ball had bounced twice before going in. She thought it didn't count as a hole-in-one unless it went in on the fly.) My wife, Amanda, parred a true par four on her first day—the fourth hole of golf she'd ever played, at the challenging Bretwood course in Keene, New Hampshire. The game is strange that way: so demanding, so exacting, so unforgiving most of the time. And then it gives away these unexpected bonuses to people who have paid no dues.

I'm grateful for that. I'll take every bonus I can get, and I like to see beginners get lucky. But there is a flip side to this aspect of golf, and it has to do with the complicated strategies of the ego.

Once, at the Mount Anthony Country Club in Bennington, Vermont, one of my favorite courses, I found myself behind a foursome of men in their seventies. I was playing alone that day and pinched for time to the point that I was hoping to get in nine holes and no more. Though I'd caught up to them when they were on the first green, these gentlemen made no move to wave me through. I waited on the second tee, a par three, and waited again on the third and fourth fairways, standing by my ball in the classic pose of polite impatience—both hands resting on the top of the grip with the club upright in front of me—while they very slowly chipped and putted. They were members, I suppose, and I was a walk-on. They were obviously friends playing in their regular foursome, perhaps for money, with no other place they needed to be. And it was late October. In Vermont, in late October, it is safe to assume that every round will be the last of the year. Still, they surely saw me standing there every time they glanced back and, since there was no one for several holes in front of them, it would have cost them only a couple of minutes' wait to wave me through. I was not pleased.

Somewhere in that stretch of holes I began to suspect it was a particular brand of the masculine ego I was witness to, and a victim of. They were good golfers, all of them. But it was easy to see that the years had taken some of the juice out of their drives and stolen a little of the lightness from their steps. It began to be clear to me that they had taken my relatively fast-paced play as some kind of silent challenge, and believed they had to rise to the occasion and prove—to themselves, to each other, and to me—that all four of them together, walking no less, could still match the younger fellow stroke for stroke, Goddammit, if need be.

I could not possibly have cared less about matching them stroke for stroke. What I cared about was finishing my nine holes of stolen, middle-of-the-workday golf and getting back in time for a one-thirty appointment. I didn't hit too close to them or make any rude remarks or gestures. When I see older golfers I feel the same as when I see older drivers behind the wheel—I hope I get there someday, and I allow them a little maneuvering room. But not pushing them too hard meant that I didn't get close enough to ask if I could play through.

The sixth hole is a 370-yard uphill par four that curves slightly to the right. By the time I reached the tee box they were 120 yards away, climbing toward their shots. I waited six or eight or ten minutes, until they'd played their approaches, then I drove, and started my own climb in their footsteps. One of them was far over in the left rough, still seventy-five yards or so from the green after his second shot. His playing partners were either on or close to being on. He was wearing a light-colored jacket, and I'd already identified him, to my own bristling satisfaction, as the slowest player in the group. I reached my ball, assumed my pose, watched. He swung and, holding his finish position as if he were being photographed for the cover of *Obnoxious Man*, studied the flight of his ball with a hopeful, proud expression. Someone shouted something I couldn't make out. Another moment and there was more shouting, a sense of celebration around the green, and my friend in the pale jacket raised his hands above his head in jubilation. He had holed out, a nice, seventy-five-yard birdie. I waited another five minutes, finished the hole with a three-putt bogey, then walked across to the ninth and headed in.

There was something familiar to me in that man's happy pose, in the way he slid his iron back into his bag and walked jauntily up to join his pals. It was more than happiness; it was triumph. It was as if he were holding that moment up to the face of someone who'd ridiculed him in fifth grade and saying, *"See."* Or as if, after all those fairly good or pretty good or quite good rounds, he believed his true golfing self had finally shown its face, and it was nothing short of masterful.

Perhaps he wasn't thinking that at all. Probably he was just some happy guy who knew he'd made a once-in-a-lifetime shot and would go home, tell his wife the good news, bask in the memory of it for the next couple of days, then move on. Probably it was his partners who were slowing things down. Probably I was even a little bit pleased for him.

But I know that, for myself, those are not only the shots that keep me coming back; they are also—like my first two strokes in the league at Edge Hill—the ones that tempt me to play outside the range of my actual abilities.

"Ego," Sogyal Rinpoche said, "is the absence of true knowledge of who we really are, together with its result: a doomed clutching on, at all costs, to a cobbled together and makeshift image of ourselves."

Perhaps that explains why the foursome refused to let me through: It would have been too hard for them to let go of their image of themselves, outdated and inaccurate though it was. And it probably also explains why I kept going for the first green at Edge Hill with my second shot when most of the time I would have scored lower if I'd played a long iron to within fifty yards and then tried to hit a wedge in close—as Walt usually did.

In fact, looking back on that season, I realize that he tried several times, in roundabout ways, to get the message to me. "That's a good move, hitting an iron from this tee," he said on the few occasions I tried it. Or, "The way you're hitting that driver sure puts a lot of pressure on your short game to make birdies." But nothing he might have said would have reached me that season. I had lost fifteen years of prime golfing time because of back troubles. Like the foursome in front of me at Mount Anthony, I was out to prove something.

But ego is a complicated beast, a sly foe. One or two great shots or great off-course successes and it praises us in some secret language, builds us up and up, momentarily convinces us that we are special, superior, a kind of treasure among human beings. Which would be fine if we were the only people on earth. Or on the course.

Ego can work from the other direction, too, cutting down instead of building up. You hit a terrible, an embarrassingly terrible shot at a key point in the match, or play an awful round or several awful rounds in a row, and the memory echoes in your thoughts until, again, you have cobbled together an image of yourself that is false and destructive. Destructive to your scoring and destructive to the hope of peace that golf offers.

Ego is usually associated only with the former problem, the triumphant passages in the inner symphony. But I think it's more accurate to see it as working both angles, aiming at a kind of interior stickiness, the place in us that holds on too tightly to praise as well as criticism—from others and from ourselves.

I've seen the world's best men and women professionals play in person, and it seems to me that, while some of them have big egos off the course, not many have big egos on it. They are pleased at their great shots and displeased by their poor ones, but they have trained themselves not to dwell too long on either—to find what Buddha called the "golden mean" between exhilaration and despair.

At the 2000 Nissan Open at Riviera, Tiger Woods four-putted a green, surely a rare moment in golf and, as the commentators noted during the replay, something we may never see again. You could tell he was displeased, as well he might be. But that displeasure did not stick to him. He made a long putt for birdie on the next hole and went on about his business.

And a few weeks later, on a breezy Saturday afternoon at the Tournament Players Championship, Hal Sutton hit his tee shot into the water on the seventeenth, took a triple bogey, and saw his comfortable four-stroke lead over Woods shrink to one. But he neatly parred the next hole and eventually won the tournament by a stroke.

The most difficult part of this battle with the ego, I think, is finding that kind of unshakable balance, tuning the instrument of self-esteem to just the right volume. Even the Dalai Lama—head of a religion that has declared all-out war on the ego—acknowledges that there are two kinds of ego, healthy and unhealthy. And Khan said that the mystic "understands that in man there is a real ego, that this ego is divine, but that the divine ego is covered by a false ego; and every man has a false ego because it begins to grow from his birth."

In order to improve we have to care, we have to try, we have to make a distinction between good shots and bad and want more of the former and less of the latter. Caring too much, though—trying too hard, paying obsessive attention to *my* swing, *my* shots, *my* score—can twist a golf game, and a person, into knots.

4

ANGER: EGO'S CHIEF OF STAFF

Even if an angry man were to revive the dead, he would not be pleasing to God because of his anger.

—Abbot Agatho

And not be pleasing to his wife or children or friends either, we might add. And not be much fun on the links.

I played a bit of golf in high school and I remember some of the guys I played with doing things like throwing clubs into ponds, wrapping them around trees, or having tantrums in which they occasionally did damage to a green with their putters. I slung a few irons, too, in those days, and ruined some afternoons because of a few bad shots.

Later in my life, while I was struggling to build a career as a writer, I worked as a self-employed carpenter for seven years. My troubles with anger were, unfortunately, as much a part of those days as my scarred old soft-soled workboots.

There is a great amount of pressure to being self-employed—more in the construction business than in some others. If you're working outdoors and it rains, you lose a day's pay. No sick days, no excuses if something goes awry. Sometimes that pressure would find the stickiest part of me and remain there, taunting and nagging until it pulled me off balance. I'd be trying to install a storm door and discover that the instructions for assembling it were written in an unclear way; or I'd be framing a wall and realize, when it was mostly done, that I'd somehow measured wrong and the windows were sitting up three inches higher than the blueprints said they should; or I'd give a customer a poor estimate and find myself three-quarters of the way through a job that was already supposed to be finished, which meant I'd be working a day or a week, or, once, several weeks, for no pay. There were moments in those years when I'd go off on strings of cursing and muttering I'd be ashamed to see on tape now. I'd stride around the worksite kicking at stones or scraps of wood, spitting, grinding teeth, making fists. I'd fling a tool or drive the head of my hammer into a two-by-six header, leaving a half-inch-deep coin-shaped monument to my temper. I was, at those moments, an ugly soul.

You find ugly souls on the golf course from time to time, even among the professional ranks. The muttering, the cursing, the blaming and headshaking. It's almost as if the body's liquids have been set to boiling, and you can see the steam rise and hear the lid of the pot clattering. It makes me think of the Ojibway song:

Sometimes I
I go about pitying
Myself
While I am carried by the wind
Across the sky.

Self-pity is surely one aspect of golf anger. Self-criticism is another. I was playing in a foursome last summer at a friend's course, and one of the other players—a good golfer and a nice guy—was having an off day. Bad shot by bad shot, you could feel the heat going up inside him. By the next-to-last hole he had already lost a match he knew he should have won, and at that point not even some good shots could bring him out of his sour mood. On the last hole he hit an errant drive—not awful by any means, but well to the right of where he wanted to be—and it set off a ten-minute tantrum. He flung his club to the ground, picked it up and slammed it into his bag. He paced back and forth, swearing, spitting, kicking the turf, standing still just long enough for the next person to hit and then starting up all over again.

Looking at him (though none of us spent much time looking at him), you could see clearly that he was angry at himself. Fair enough: He'd blown his match, played far below his ability. But it was the degree of anger that seemed wrong, unbalanced, out of all proportion to his errors. On that day there was a large distance between the way the world was and the way he insisted it should be: which might serve as a definition of the territory anger occupies.

I couldn't help but think back to my carpentry tantrums. At least my golfing friend was blaming himself, whereas I started out blaming the person who wrote the storm-door assembly directions, or the guy at the lumberyard who'd sold me crooked two-by-fours, or the customer for being so fussy, and only eventually graduated to the point of "driving all blames into one."

In my case, and I suspect in my friend's, the anger had roots buried at a level much deeper than the immediate problem, roots going back to the previous weeks and years and even far back into childhood. Unrealistic expectations, a need for perfection, a history of criticism that led to a habit of self-criticism. You can't always see those things in an angry golfer, or in yourself when you are the angry golfer, but I believe they are always there, just as a certain kind of geological history and certain conditions and elements are always part of a volcanic eruption.

Eventually, the carpentry tantrums led me to The Theory of Thirty-two Degrees. The Theory of Thirty-two Degrees begins with the fact that, under ordinary circumstances, water turns to ice at thirty-two degrees Fahrenheit. God doesn't stand there waiting for the thermometer to drop to thirty-two and then go around waving a magic wand at all the standing water in the area. The water doesn't care whether you want it to freeze or not, whether you've been good or not. It just freezes. It's a law of life. Another law of life is this: If you get your thumb between the hammer and the wood, you will hit your thumb with the hammer and it will hurt. There is, as Marlon Brando said in *The Godfather*, "nothing personal" about it. The fates are not out to get you. You are not cursed. You are not the miserably unlucky person to whom bad things always happen for no reason. You just had your thumb in the wrong place. You just hit your shot wrong.

> *Sometimes I*
> *I go about pitying*
> *Myself*
> *While I am carried by the wind*
> *Across the sky.*

To form a model of the world with *I* at the center, a target for the archer of bad luck, is to fall victim to one of the ego's sly strategies. Certainly there is a capricious element involved in what happens on a golf course; certainly luck plays a role in our score (though not in our handicap), just as it plays a role in what happens to us elsewhere in life. But even if it isn't true that good breaks and bad breaks balance each other out, I think it's wise to pretend that it's true.

The most outrageous example of golfing luck I've ever heard of happened on a course a few miles from my house. The fourth hole there is a short par three that presses up close against a two-lane state highway. There are probably ten yards between the back of the green and the edge of the road, a stretch of land planted with shrubs and heavy grass. Two summers ago someone teed off there with the wrong club and sent his ball flying up and into the highway. The ball hit a passing vehicle, then caromed back onto the green and into the hole for what is probably the most unusual hole-in-one in golf history. The golfer was invited to appear on the Jay Leno show, and Leno paid for the damage to the vehicle.

All of us have seen similar, if more probable, touches of luck—good and bad. A nice drive bounces ninety degrees sideways and ends up in a ditch, or a putt is stopped just short of the hole by a tiny blemish on the green, or, at a pivotal moment in the tournament, the second shot on a par five comes to rest in a divot. I once lost a key hole in a match to someone whose short putt, pushed two inches off line, bumped my ball marker and angled back into the cup.

But we've all hit tee shots into the trees and watched them bounce out into the middle of the fairway, or skimmed shots off the surface of a water hole and out again, or completely mishit a chip shot and watched it race across the putting surface, knock hard against the pin, and disappear into the hole.

It may be a good idea to carry around in the bag, like an extra club, the theory that luck balances out; that if you get a couple of bad breaks in a round, it means you're due for some good breaks later on. And it helps to give as much attention to good fortune as to bad. If nothing else, this works to eliminate self-pity, one of the pillars on which the anger palace is built.

Luck is a very small part of the game, really. Those quirky shots aside, it's best to abide by The Theory of

Thirty-two Degrees. If your ball slices, you made an out-side-in swing, period. The laws of golf are as unvarying as the laws of physics. In fact, they *are* the laws of physics. And they will not change for you no matter how good you've been to your children, how much money you've made, or how powerful a personality you have. Surely no amount of anger will change them.

In searching out the roots of anger, it is useful to listen to the kinds of things we say to ourselves during a bad moment on the course. "You bum, you idiot. How could you be so *stupid?* You are *always* doing *stupid, idiotic* things like this. What is the *matter* with you?" Or: "This always happens to me. Just when I'm playing good, I get a lousy break like that. Did you see that? Can you believe that? This *always* happens!"

One of the beautiful aspects of golf is the way it peels the coating away from the habitual run of our thoughts, the way it reveals the hidden layers of who we think we are, how we tell ourselves the world works. It resembles meditation in this way, and it resembles marriage. For showing us both the flimsy and solid places in our own inner architecture, there is nothing better than sitting quietly for an hour and watching our thoughts . . . unless it is living with another person for a few decades . . . or having a bad day on the links.

In this sense, anger on the course is an opportunity, a message-containing bottle knocking up against the hull of the boat. When we've calmed down a bit we can fish the bottle out and open it; we can examine the outburst and see what might have prepared the ground for it. Or not. The other option is to tell ourselves it's a sign of our fiercely competitive nature, or give examples of great tennis or football players who use anger to motivate themselves or intimidate their opponents, and then continue to spew vitriol into the air around our playing partners. After all, the pros have tantrums sometimes, too, don't they? Yes, rarely. But in any case, the real goal of golf is not to play like the pros.

Strange as it may seem, the real goal may be to play like an eighty-seven-year-old. One of the aspects I most appreciate about playing in the men's league at Worthington is the opportunity to spend time with golfers in different stages of life. (The ages of the members in the league range from mid-twenties to early nineties.) The senior golfers are all different, naturally—some outgoing and some quiet, some confident and some uncertain, some low handicappers, some high. With very few exceptions, though, they exhibit a sort of dignified mellowness. I have never seen one of them throw a club or go off on a tantrum, cursing his luck.

The lowest round I shot last summer was a solitary round—I like to play alone once a week if I can. On the third hole I ended up behind an eighty-seven-year-old man who is a frequent visitor to the club. He was playing alone, too, but using a cart. He didn't see me behind him, and, though he wasn't dawdling, his pace of play was very slow. It was a sunny, quiet weekday afternoon, with few other people on the course. Instead of moving up close and getting in position to pass—which is what I usually would have done—I held back, reminded myself I had no particular place to get to that day, and tried to adjust myself to his pace. Playing at his speed, letting go of the need to be efficient, I found a deep, unfamiliar calm settling over me. It was impossible to be angry at anything. I had plenty of time to consider my shots, and if I did hit one poorly, I was checked from my natural impulse to hurry after the offending hook or slice and quickly make amends. For an hour or so I was playing like an eighty-seven-year-old, being that deliberate, and shooting the best golf of my life. I started trying to recapture that feeling on other days, a sort of rock-solid imperturbability—as if any given round might be my last, and I ought at least to enjoy it.

We read and hear often about players who had a bad temper in their younger days but grew out of it. I don't know why it works that way. Maybe anger is connected to speed, and as we slow down it naturally weakens. Maybe it's hormonal. Maybe, over time, most of us just come to see its counterproductive nature, the way it corrodes marriages and friendships, confuses children, spoils what could have been an enjoyable afternoon on the links. Maybe we should ask our course elders to go around the country giving seminars on the subject, passing on, to the young and the middle aged, the secrets of their self-discipline and calm.

5

ETIQUETTE: THE LANGUAGE OF GRACE

And silence, like a poultice, comes
To heal the blows of sound.

—Oliver Wendell Holmes,
"The Music Grinder"

L ast September the Ryder Cup was played here in Massachusetts—at The Country Club in Brookline, just outside Boston—and I was lucky enough to have a generous friend with two tickets for the final day's matches. After the matches were over we walked out of the gates in a boisterous, happy crowd, found Bob's car, and set about getting lost on Brookline's quiet streets. I turned on the radio and tuned in to a sports talk show on which the hosts were discussing the drama of the individual matches. As most golfers know, that Sunday was one of the most magical days in American sports history—the U.S. team coming back from a 10–6 deficit to regain the cup by a margin of $14\frac{1}{2}$ to $13\frac{1}{2}$. But the sports commentator wasn't focusing on that.

"Michael Jordan has to make a free throw in front of thirty thousand fans who are swearing at him, yelling, flipping him the bird, waving their arms," he said. Then, in a very sarcastic tone: "But, oh my, Colin Montgomerie or Tom Lehman is about to putt. *Shh*, everybody. God forbid there's a little movement or noise in the gallery. This is *golf*, after all."

Golf, I wanted to tell him through the radio, is different. Golf is all about silence.

"In silence," said Meister Eckehart, "man can most readily preserve his integrity."

But silence, exterior as well as interior, is a rare ore in the modern world. Sometimes I wonder if we have mined it into extinction already—if there was a given supply at the beginning of time and it has been depleted over the centuries, leaving us condemned to a purgatory of ceaseless noise. Golf is one of the last fortresses of silence, and it irritated me but didn't really surprise me to hear it coming under assault by someone who talks and argues for a living.

A society's games—like its art, its leaders, its architecture—act as a mirror for the society itself. In the 1960s and

'70s, when I was playing ice hockey, it was a wonderful game. It's still a great sport at the high school and college level. But for me at least, professional hockey has been ruined. As the saying goes: "I went to the fights and a hockey game broke out." It was always a rough sport—roughness is part of the fun—but there is a clear line between roughness and violence, and too often now pro hockey obviously crosses it: bare-knuckle fights, head-butts, the stick used as a lethal weapon. There are brawls in baseball and basketball, too—fans seem drawn to them. I wonder how long it will be before we see fights on the PGA tour, Duval and Parnevik duking it out, literally, at Augusta.

It's comforting to stand back and wag a pious finger at this increased tolerance for violence: Not long ago it was a hot issue in the press, and there was a spray of commentary on the subject. But perhaps it's of more value to try to find the roots of that behavior in ourselves, to examine the breach of interior silence that spawns it.

On the last day of the 2000 Phoenix Open Hal Sutton was booed and heckled because of some comments he'd made to the press the day before about the unruly crowd. The heckling appeared to affect his game. Before he reached the beer-drinking mob at the sixteenth hole, he was tied for the lead and, as commentator Ken Venturi noted, seemed to be "in the zone." After the heckling at the sixteenth, his concentration wavered, and he ended up finishing in a three-way tie for fourth.

This behavior was reminiscent of the rough job some Ryder Cup fans did on Colin Montgomerie—in the name of patriotism, perhaps, or because the jeers always upset him so much. And in a kind of reverse patriotism Tiger Woods was heckled and loudly rooted against by some fans at the 1999 PGA Championship at Medinah—because they'd taken a sudden liking to the charismatic style of Sergio Garcia.

Woods, Sutton, and Montgomerie are among the very best golfers in the world—obviously the jeering has nothing to do with the quality of their games. And it has little to do with their characters, either. It's all about jealousy, all about the rude fans' feeling of smallness in the world. (Why else would someone yell out, "In the hole!" as loudly as possible one-tenth of a second after Tiger's driver makes contact with the ball, except that he wants his girlfriend back home to hear and recognize his voice on television?) Fans heckle great athletes because, like second-graders left out of an adult conversation, they want to feel included, feel as though the spotlight is on them, too. This particular kind of insecurity is a side effect of our obsession with celebrity. For people who feel small and inconsequential in their own lives, the attention paid to star athletes is salt in the wound. They believe the only remedy for the pain is noise—when in fact it's silence.

Silence is a threatening creature. I remember walking around in Moscow's Park of Economic Achievements on a sunny summer day in 1987. The park was a type of low-key world's fair. There were buildings holding exhibits of the Soviet Union's technological achievements, paths, fountains, families strolling along licking ice cream cones. A nice domestic scene, except that a government radio station was blaring propaganda at top volume from speakers set up on the lightpoles. It was as if the Soviet leaders worried that their citizens might fill in any silent moments with a bit of independent thinking.

We are not so different. We may not be subjected to a constant barrage of messages telling us how we must think and behave (unless you count advertisement as propaganda), but in cities especially, there is an obvious trend toward filling in whatever silent moments still exist. Muzak in elevators, music piped into the air over department store and drugstore aisles, TV screens in gyms, on tour buses. Walkmans, cell phones, beeping watches, pagers—we wait in line for a fast-food hamburger and are subjected to the calls and cries of kitchen machinery, a cacophony of toots, squeaks, and whistles, then carry our food outside only to be forced to listen to music blasting out of car windows and antitheft alarms whirring and hooting in the parking lot. Since the invention of the scanner, even libraries are louder. The silence of the shore is broken by the whine of jet skis, the silence of the winter woods by the drone of snowmobiles.

The golf course is one of a very small number of places where we can be assured of some measure of quiet. There is the soft splutter of cart engines, perhaps a single triumphant shout from a distant green, but these are sporadic, mild disturbances in a blanket of natural quiet. This precious silence is an enormous part of why we associate golf with peace and relaxation.

From Buddha to Thoreau, mystics insist that stillness and silence are the cornerstones of human happiness. They aren't interested in quiet for its own sake, and have nothing, I would bet, against a little movement now and then. Their insistence comes from an intuitive understanding of how we use noise and constant motion to run away from the workings of our own mind. Pascal said, "All human evil comes from this, man's being unable to sit still in a room." If we manage to find a quiet moment, and a quiet place, and sit for even a few minutes without doing anything, this statement comes to seem more and more profound. We become aware of a disturbing interior din. Some of it is productive thinking, a logical working-out of important problems.

Most of it is just chatter. The mystics say union with the Divine is what lies beyond the curtain of this chatter. Which is a nice coincidence, because champion golfers say that this is where their best golf games are, too.

I was on the eighth fairway at Worthington last summer, playing with a friend who was having one of those days when, tee to green, every shot is a struggle. "Too much thinking," he said to himself, aloud. "Not enough paying attention." The pros say similar things about the secret of their games, though they couch their wisdom in more oblique terms. They talk about learning to "immediately forget a bad shot," "having no swing thoughts," "blocking out all distractions," "being in the zone," "visualizing," or "thinking only of the target," but what they are really talking about is finding a way, a trick, of getting past the curtain of thoughts and playing from a place of interior quiet. Thinking less, and paying attention more. Accomplished athletes in all sports know the route into this quiet territory, whether they play in front of thirty thousand jeering fans or thirty thousand absolutely silent ones. You can see the light of it in their faces, as if they are mirrors reflecting a quiet, still universe, or as if they have managed to hold a part of themselves completely immobile while their bodies are in motion. Ted Williams claimed he could see the seams of the baseball as it came toward him at ninety-five miles an hour. In some cases it is a gift, a rare capacity for concentration that the greatest athletes, and greatest spiritual masters, have from birth. More often it is a skill developed by thousands of hours of practice. (In fact, Buddhist masters often use the word *practice* where others say *prayer* or *meditation*.) "Study to be quiet," Izaak Walton said in *The Compleat Angler*. What an odd concept this is in a civilization in which machines fill the workplace with a constant electric hum; in which we go out for a walk in the park with music clamped over our ears, and use the constant chatter of radio or TV not just for information, amusement, or companionship, but because we have abandoned all hope of any real interior rest. *Study to be quiet:* That radical idea works as well on the course as it does in the trout stream.

Golf can give us a graphic demonstration of the state of our inner weather. While some days are good or bad for no apparent reason, at other times we can see different degrees of interior turmoil reflected in our swing. Sometimes all it takes is one flubbed chip shot to bring this turmoil to the surface. The skim coating of equilibrium is sliced open and all sorts of worry and trouble come bubbling forth: anger, anxiousness, money and domestic woes—all the things we go to the course to forget about in the first place. We can then become more upset—because we're supposed to be out here having a good time, and that chip shot ruined the hole, the round, the whole vacation. Really, though, all it did was reveal what is actually going on in our inner world. As a friend of mine, a Trappist monk, said, about the thoughts that arise in meditation, "Those things come up in order to be relaxed."

On good days we play from a quiet center, and this relaxation occurs without effort. Thoughts don't bubble up as we address the ball, the swing feels natural and smooth, the putting stroke is untroubled. The day has a silent shine to it, and the pleasure of the course follows us home and lights up the rest of the afternoon.

It's not easy to learn the technique of keeping this peace with us on more difficult days, of relaxing rather than feeding the turmoil—on the course or off it. Most of the mystics quoted here spent decades disciplining themselves away from distraction and toward peace. They went on solitary retreats, spent hours in contemplation, read, studied, prayed, fasted, gave up sex, gave up meat, even gave up golf in their pursuit of deeper joys. We may not want to carry things to that extent, but cultivating the silent interior gardens within us is an option available to anyone in the context of any life. It is possible to practice silence as we practice tee shots or seven-irons; to study it, as Walton said, to learn its laws the way we learn the grammar of any other language. When we hit a bad shot, or feel a burst of aggravation coming on at home, instead of going with the inertia of the emotion—which almost always leads to more trouble—we can practice learning to diffuse it. We can look for that silence and let it break the angry momentum. Without ignoring a problem that needs to be dealt with, or sugarcoating difficulties, we can take a breath and reach into that reserve of quiet—"make your mind big," as Sogyal Rinpoche put it—rather than confine it in anger's narrow trough. Sometimes one breath is all it takes to choose calm over fury. Often I can't manage to do this—the habit of a bad temper dies slowly—but I have never yet managed it and had it hurt my game. This is part of the greatness of golf. It shows us these troubles and lets us work them out on the course, lets us *practice* there, in an arena where, really, the price for failure is low.

Unlike most other sports, there is no such thing as "playing defense" in golf. The rules of etiquette stand as a clear proof that golf is primarily about learning to conquer ourselves—our tempers, interior noises, and lapses in concentration—and not about conquering our opponent. Good etiquette means more than being quiet at the proper time, or playing at a reasonable pace; it means giving opponents every opportunity to play their best. Which is the exact opposite of what goes on with heckling crowds. Like marathon running, like yoga, like marriage, golf is all about mastering the self. Being silent and still when the opponent is playing, observing the correct order of teeing off and putting, even taking a moment to replace a divot, rake the sand in a bunker, or toss a bit of gravel off the putting surface—this kind of behavior feeds a well of dignity and patience within us. Who knows when we might have to draw from it?

But this is the kind of behavior the talk-show host, the worst fans, and the most obnoxious golfers themselves scorn. Apparently they would prefer a sport of trash-talkers, brawlers, and role models who want victory at any cost. They want golf to be played in a coliseum atmosphere—which corresponds, I suppose, to the fearful noise they experience if they try to sit somewhere quietly for an hour.

6

THE DRAGONS OF FEAR

You gain strength, courage, and confidence by every experience in which you really stop to look fear in the face.

—Anna Eleanor Roosevelt, "You Learn by Living"

One side effect of playing golf is that it reveals the fear within us. This might seem, at first glance, like a peculiar assertion, since the element of danger that looms so large in many sports is all but nonexistent in golf. Every year golfers are killed by lightning, and we've all heard stories of someone being struck by a golf ball and blinded or badly hurt, but there isn't the constant threat of a crippling injury that one faces in rugby, football, or ice hockey, nor the kind of pain that comes from the extreme exertion of rowing, cycling, long-distance swimming, or running. But fear comes packaged in different shapes: physical, emotional, psychological; fear of heights, fear of intimacy, fear of change. In each of its manifestations it encircles a piece of our life like a berm of concertina wire. Golf shines a spotlight on these barriers, at least, and in some cases shows us a route through.

Fear of humiliation is probably the most common fear encountered on the course. Though it takes various forms, it affects golfers across the whole spectrum of ability—from professionals to first-timers. Some people are so intimidated by this fear that, despite the encouragement and protestations of their most trusted advisers, they won't venture onto the course at all. Some of my women friends whose husbands are avid golfers, and who have spent years listening to their spouses' stories of glory and defeat, are afraid to take up the game for fear of being embarrassed in front of their mates, of seeming foolish or dumb. Some of them grew up in an era when only a small percentage of schoolgirls participated in sports, and they labor under the illusion that hitting a golf ball a hundred yards down a fairway is a feat of athleticism far beyond them.

I have men friends with this attitude, too. Somewhere in their childhood they were embarrassed at not being as coordinated as their schoolmates in baseball or basketball.

They assume golf must require the same types of skills. They have a mental image of themselves standing on a tee and missing the ball completely, repeatedly, to a chorus of nasty guffaws from scratch players sipping gin-and-tonics on the clubhouse porch. (A fly-fishing friend says he's noted a sharp increase in the numbers of very aggressive, competitive young fly fishers who make fun of less talented, less experienced older fishermen, but I have not yet noticed a trend toward such behavior on the golf course.) The price of this fear is that they miss out on one of life's greatest pleasures, and never give themselves the opportunity to break free from their own negative image of themselves.

Even for professionals at the top of the sport, there are plenty of chances for humiliation. In a way, the fear is even greater at that level, since so much more is expected of them, and since they are almost always playing in front of an audience. The history of professional golf is littered with tales of last-round collapses, missed two-foot putts on the eighteenth hole, famous flubbed wedge shots—legends of disgrace that will remain etched into the mind of fans for a generation before time erases them. Jean Van de Velde and his valiant collapse at the 1999 British Open come readily to mind: Thanks to very poor judgment, an aversion to playing it safe, and then an unlucky bounce, he blew a three-stroke lead on the final hole and lost the tournament in a playoff. In his case, however, the humiliation has been softened somewhat by the way he dealt with it—blaming no one but himself, making no excuses, coming right back the next week to try again.

More than most sports, golf provides an abundance of opportunity for that kind of embarrassment. It is so absolutely individualistic, for one thing. For another, the failures and errors are often exceedingly dramatic: sending a white ball flying a hundred yards into a still pond, where the waves spread and carom off the banks for long seconds afterward; hitting a shot that trickles off the tee in a shower of turf, or squirts onto another fairway, or pops sideways into the flower beds next to the clubhouse restaurant where your spouse, children, in-laws, and next-door neighbors—people who have been listening to you talk about the glories of golf for years—are sitting and watching, waiting for you to finish your game so you can come join them for a birthday dinner. Striking out in a company softball game compares to this?

And something about the size of the ball—a few ounces next to our hundred- or two-hundred-pound bulk—makes a flubbed shot seem so pathetic, the golfer so pitiful and inept. Something about the obvious simplicity of tapping a ball three feet along very smooth grass into a four-and-a-quarter-inch hole makes missing a putt that much worse. Then, too, in golf there is not the enforced distance between player and spectator that one finds in most other sports. At least when you strike out in baseball, or when a pro tennis star whiffs on her opponent's serve, there is a small cushion of space between the stands and the playing surface, a few dozen square yards of air in which to take refuge. In golf, your opponents or playing partners are standing so close to you on the tee that you can hear their wristwatches ticking. For the PGA tour player who hits into the rough alongside a green, the next shot will have to be played in front of a gallery of spectators standing three club lengths away.

I play golf often with my wife, Amanda. And at least a few times a season we manage to get out in a threesome with my mother, Eileen. Both women are avid golfers and fun to be around on the course. One year we couldn't bear to wait for spring so we flew south in late February, with our infant daughter Alexandra, and spent four days at a resort called Sea Trail on the southernmost part of the coast of North Carolina. There we established a fair rotation: One of us minded Alexandra while the other two played. On the day I was playing with my mother we were booked for the Maples course, and since it was the off season and a quiet time of day, and since the first tee was only a hundred yards from our condominium, Amanda brought the baby and the videocamera along, hoping to record the moment for posterity. The baby was in her stroller, half asleep, Amanda standing fifteen feet behind me, camera on. Just at the top of my backswing our daughter let out a chirping noise, a cute little sound no father could fail to be moved by. The problem was that I was so moved I missed the ball. Actually, I didn't quite miss it; I grazed it with the heel of my driver just enough that it toppled off the wooden tee and rolled a few inches along the fine Carolina grass, coming to rest near the toe of my left shoe. We have the moment perfectly preserved on tape. Some days, when I have played better than I usually do and feel my head swelling, I imagine our daughter showing that clip to her children thirty or forty years down the road. "See, honey. That was your grandfather. And that's golf, the game he loved."

Perhaps it was an inherited blunder. My father liked to tell the story of the second or third time he ever played, at a public course just north of Boston. The first tee was surrounded by regulars waiting to hit their drives. It was the usual scene—jokes, impatience, men zipping up the pockets of their golf bags and tugging at the cuffs of their gloves. They went silent when he addressed the ball. He was a big man, and he swung, hard, and missed it completely. More silence, a cough from the gallery. He stared down at the offending white sphere, looked up at his audience, and said, "Tough course."

Eventually, if we play honestly enough, through enough humiliations, if we practice with our fears in a disciplined way, we get worn down to what Zen teachers call our "true self" or our "true face," or perhaps in this context "our true golfing face." The degree to which we fear humiliation is the distance we still have to go to find our true golfing face, because, just as anger is often a sign of resistance to the present facts, humiliation is resisting the truth of who we actually are at any given moment, a way of saying no to one of the many facets of the spirit we call "I."

This kind of resistance, this kind of fear can be measured by the number of excuses made: the wind, the lie, the grips, the clubs, the course design or condition, the argument we had with our wife/husband/boss just before teeing off. A part of us is willing to reach for any excuse rather than face that last number on the right-hand edge of the scorecard. I would have shot seventy if the greens weren't so slow. Okay, that may be true. But the greens are what they are, and you shot 76 or 86 or 126. On this day, at least, that is your golf game there in those numbers.

Which brings me to the subject of cheating.

Before approaching this uncomfortable area, I think it's best to pause a moment and repeat something that was said earlier: There's room under the golf umbrella for all sorts of attitudes. Some people go out on the course every week or two when the weather is good, whack at the ball, smoke a cigar, tell a few jokes, enjoy a drink with friends in the clubhouse afterward, then return to the rest of their life satisfied and refreshed. They are as much a part of the beauty of golf as is the two-handicapper who has his swing speed measured every spring and breaks out a new balata on every third hole. Members of the former group avail themselves of what a friend of mine calls "the magnificent mulligan" after chunking a tee shot into the pond. They prop the ball up in the rough to get a pretty lie. They use an illegal tee or illegal grips and carry sixteen or eighteen clubs. God bless them.

Cheating is something else. Cheating is when a player does those things and then pretends—to himself and to others—that his score means something. Cheating is when he keeps an official handicap but doesn't enter certain rounds into the computer; when she conveniently forgets a penalty stroke and hopes she won't be reminded; when, having hit into the woods in match play, he nudges the ball an inch or two out from behind that tree. I think of Jordan Baker in *The Great Gatsby,* probably golf's most famous cheater. There was something veiled and false about her, a type of arrogance coupled with the fear that she might turn out to be something less than she appeared to be.

Cheating, like compulsive making of excuses, is a species of fear, a stubborn, sly resistance to the truth of ourselves. As Krishnamurti said, "We are always comparing what we are with what we should be."

The other type of fear encountered on the golf course is something much subtler and perhaps even more limiting than the fear of failure or embarrassment, and that is the fear of success. This, too, can be read as easily in the game of the touring professional as in that of the average player. Some pros play week after week and year after year on the tour, collecting top-ten finishes—and never winning. Or they lead the big tournament until the last two holes, then hand it over to someone else. This could be because they have, in fact, reached the upper limit of their abilities, or because they fold under the pressure of the PGA tour—a pressure so intense it is impossible for the nonprofessional to imagine. But it could also be due to the fact that success is frightening to them in some way. It was nice to watch Kirk Triplett win at Riviera this spring after eleven years on the tour and 266 starts without a victory. Even his nearest rival, Jesper Parnevik, said he was rooting for him. You could see him falter in the final stretch, pulling his drive into the rough at a crucial moment, as if he were afraid of stepping into the winner's circle. Then you could see him conquer that fear, put his game back together, make a nice shot out of the rough, and finish with a slippery four-foot putt to beat Parnevik on the seventy-second hole.

As subtle as this fear of success is, it is nevertheless easy to track. The place to look for it is on the eleventh or twelfth hole when we've played the front nine in two strokes less than our previous best. At this point some of us will notice ourselves waiting for the other shoe to drop, for disaster to strike. And in golf, as in other aspects of living, nothing invites disaster better than expecting it.

For me, this fear was most noticeable before I broke forty for the first time, for nine holes. For years, because of back problems, I had either not played at all or played just a handful of times every summer. I didn't have an official handicap, but it must have been close to thirty. Playing this way, I became accustomed to disaster, even went on the course expecting it. There would be some pars, a rare birdie, but there would also be sevens, eights, nines, and tens. In a certain strange way I had taught myself to get more pleasure from attempting the spectacular, low-percentage shot out of the trees than from playing a quiet, steady game, because those kinds of recovery shots were my little opportunities for heroism in an otherwise decidedly unheroic round.

When my back improved rather suddenly one year I began to devote more time to golf. I was in my forties by then, and playing with my father's set of ancient Ben Hogan blades and woods. It was late to get serious about golf, but what I lacked in youth I hoped to make up for in dedication.

I bought new irons and woods, not very expensive but more forgiving. I read books written by professional golfers and famous coaches. I joined a club, took lessons, spent time on the driving range and practice green, played three times a week. On the advice of two low-handicap friends I bought a lob wedge and began to focus more on my short game. Partly from watching other golfers, partly from listening to our pro, partly from reading about and studying the swings of the best players, I made some changes: started setting up a few inches farther away from the ball on my tee shots, turned my left wrist over earlier in the backswing, made a point of hitting sharply down with my middle and short irons. I adopted a more sensible and conservative approach to course management, and studied the green more carefully before putting.

My scores moved slowly but steadily downward. By the early part of the summer I had broken ninety for the first time in my life; two weeks later I shot eighty-five. I began to feel more comfortable on the course, and to start to shed my old heroic strategies. Though I had not yet come close to breaking eighty, I set myself the goal of breaking forty for nine holes—figuring it was easier to put together a half round of good play than a full one. I took a second lesson with the pro at Worthington, Erik Tiele, and shot forty-one. Over the next month I had five forty-twos and another forty-one. At the end of July and the beginning of August I shot forty, three times.

I'd get off to a good start, play six or seven solid holes, then run into a stretch of trouble that kept me in the forties. This trouble was only distantly related to my earlier disasters. I didn't drive a ball into the forest then try to hit a magnificent five-wood out, only to have the shot crack into the trunk of a pine tree and carom back over my head into the ferns, from where I would play a three-wood and dribble it out into the deep rough. It was more a case of missing a couple of short putts, or scoring a double bogey on the next-to-last hole.

But there was a thread linking my new game with my old. Three times I was lying thirty-eight on the ninth green with makeable putts that stopped within two inches of the hole or skidded just past. It began to be clear to me that I was physically ready to break forty, but not mentally ready, that while I had mostly gotten rid of some bad old habits—big slices off the tee, timid lag putts—the remnants of my old mind-set remained. In much the same way that a person who has lost a lot of weight she has been carrying around for years still pictures herself as heavy, I still had a subconscious image of myself as the golfer I had been instead of the golfer I was. I would hit the first three greens in regulation then find myself thinking: "Now watch me mess up." It was not quite as clear as that, of course; I couldn't actually hear myself thinking those words. But the thought lurked quietly in the shadows and had an obvious effect on my game.

Becoming aware of a thought pattern like that is the start of change, but not the same as changing. It wasn't for another week that I finally broke forty. Ironically, that round came at a more difficult course, but I wasn't keeping my own score and didn't know I'd shot a thirty-eight on the back nine until the round was over. The next week I broke eighty for the first time and then slipped backward for a while, as if the temperature, even at that moderately proficient level of golf, was too intense for me and I was afraid of being burned.

At one point that summer I remember reading an interview with David Duval, who recounted some advice his father had given him: "Don't be afraid to shoot low."

Don't be afraid to shoot low. It sounds like such an odd thing to be afraid of until we see the dozens of little ways that we lock our present selves into past patterns, setting limits that are purely arbitrary. It's a kind of addiction, a seeking of comfort in the repetition of old behaviors long after those behaviors have ceased giving us any real pleasure.

Talking or writing about these matters is as easy as fantasizing our way through a subpar round the night before a tournament. But anyone familiar with addictive patterns knows they have roots in the deepest soil of the psyche. The pattern will disappear for a while, then return, blind to the damage it does, fueled by a masochistic momentum that is all but unstoppable. One of the subtlest—and sometimes one of the most destructive—addictions we can have is the addiction to a lack of inner quiet. It is similar to the subtle addiction to golf disasters. On some days it seems that the world as we know it has been built simply to feed this constant urge for news, change, distraction. Some people find, even on vacation, even in a long-anticipated retirement, that they are ill at ease without some measure of the frenzy they've grown accustomed to. Like a helpful new medication that has a troublesome side effect, the technological advances of the last few decades have resulted in a lessening of patience, and in the sense that we must do several things at once to avoid falling behind. Most of us have played golf with someone who rushed from one shot to the next, putted out of turn, picked his ball out of the cup and stood at the apron of the green, ready to move on. I have friends who shave on the way to work, who read the newspaper while driving on the Massachusetts Turnpike, who curse and stamp their feet, urging the microwave display to count down the seconds more quickly. Once, in a moment of modern panic brought on by an overload of writing and teaching work, I found myself at a red light wondering if it made sense to try to read a paragraph of the book sitting beside me on the passenger seat before the light turned green again.

We are so thoroughly surrounded by rush and noise that it has come to feel like our natural state. It has invaded even that bastion of peace, the golf course. For years, business and golf have commingled on the course; the difference now, since the proliferation of cell phones, is that the two don't blend as smoothly as they once did. Perhaps there is no way around it, though Lao-tzu said,

Always be busy,
And life is beyond hope.

7

THE JOURNEY TOWARD HUMILITY

The only wisdom we can hope to acquire
Is the wisdom of humility; humility is endless.

—T. S. Eliot

Golf is a wonderful spiritual master because it edges us continually in the direction of humility. Merciless game that it is, it makes you stand there on the first tee with your pulse thumping and your friends or opponents watching in total silence. There is nowhere to hide. You can't lateral the ball off to a teammate, you can't blame the referee. If someone defeats you in match play, it is most often a slow, drawn-out defeat, a series of errors and missed chances stretched over several hours. At the end you have to watch silently and helplessly one final time as his putt drops into the hole, or as yours rolls past it, and then you have to walk up to him and shake hands.

Losing, or what ABC's *Wide World of Sports* calls "the agony of defeat," is a part of other sports, too, of course, and of many nonathletic activities. It is, I think, an aspect of competition we are afraid to talk about lest we be accused of not wanting to win badly enough. So much fuss is made over winning, so much attention lavished upon talented athletes from such an early age, that they can begin to think of themselves as superior to other people because of their ability to kick, hit, or throw. A certain amount of notice has been given lately to men in whom this arrogance becomes not just obnoxious but criminal: assault, rape, even murder. Especially in sports that demand a great deal of physical courage, winning can occasionally breed this kind of fatal conceit.

But not much attention is given to the fact that sports, on any level and at any age, can also be a route to humility. No one likes to lose. No one puts in thousands of hours of practice in order to fail. But every athlete loses at one point or another, usually hundreds of times in a career. And there is a way in which trying as hard as we can possibly try, and still failing, deflates the exaggerated false picture we have of ourselves, cuts our sweetest conceits off at the knee. Sometimes it is the most violent sports that breed the deepest humility. I will always remember Muhammad Ali's gracious response to defeat, seconds after his loss to Michael Spinks. Howard Cosell climbed into the ring and pushed a microphone in his face. "Muhammad, what happened?" he said. Ali was bruised and exhausted, witness to the public disappearance of his amazing gifts. His answer was immediate, untainted by excuses: "It was the will of Allah."

Sometimes the most conceited, most arrogant people (and the quickest to mock great competitors) are the ones who do not try at all, who let their fears keep them in the armchair, safely outside the fray, wallowing in a dream of their own imaginary splendor.

Golf is especially adept at cutting through those false dreams, because performance is measured empirically. In hockey we can have a great game—defensively, say—in ways that can't be measured. In tennis we can blow a point and still have the game marked down in our column, the blown point unrecorded. In golf every point is recorded, every miss, half miss, and mental error, every swing over the three and four days of the tournament. Sure, it sometimes happens that we hook a drive into the deep rough and then make a tremendous recovery shot and save par, or rescue an awful putting day with good ball striking. More often, though, our flaws and failures are set down with absolutely mathematical clearness. In another sport we can describe ourselves as beginners, fair players, or very good, and perhaps take some liberties. In golf we have a handicap, and it places us, to the tenth of a point, in exact relation to others who play the same game.

The potential for embarrassment shadows a golfer all the way around the course. No amount of practice or previous success renders us immune to it. No string of splendid approach shots can guarantee that the five-iron to the green with the biggest gallery won't fly off into the trees like a terrified sparrow. The only escape from it is no escape. As Lao-tzu said: "Accept disgrace willingly."

This has a nice ring to it . . . in the abstract. In fact, though, if disgrace consists of catching a ten-yard chip shot thin and shooting it well beyond the green and into deep rough, then flying the ball out of the rough and back over the green in the opposite direction while the other two members of the threesome wait near the flag, then dribbling the ball onto the apron and taking three putts to find the hole, the words *accept* and *willingly* will probably not be the first ones heard from the passionate golfer. Lao-tzu also said, "That which is cast down must first be raised," a kind of sideways hint about how to prepare for such eventualities.

The difficulty with Taoist humility, as far as golf is concerned, is that a certain amount of confidence is needed in order to perform well, a certain amount of ego even, a certain degree of belief in our own abilities. It is a kind of tightrope act, a balancing on what the Bhagavad Gita called "the razor's edge." The trick is to learn to be perfectly small yet not quite invisible in the world—something that has the feel of a lifelong project. Walking the course cloaked in false humility is no help: The *I* is still large in our picture of the world. It's just as destructive to go around listening to an internal song that has lyrics like: How wonderful I am to be so modest, how special.

Often we play our best rounds when we learn to get out of our own way, when the focus remains on the ball and where we want it to go, and not so much on our failure or success. The professional pitcher Orel Hersheiser once advised the professional golfer Paul Stankowski: "Focus on execution, not results," which is another way of saying the same thing—an indirect way of suggesting that the only place embarrassment or failure can reside in us is in the sticky material of the ego.

There are enough books on golf techniques to fill a small-town library, and they all insist that the golfer who wants to improve must put in hours of practice. There are millions of golfers, this one included, who read those books and spend hours and hours and hours trying to train ourselves to keep our right elbow close to our body on the downswing, or our head still when we putt, or, on the backswing, to twist our left shoulder all the way around in front of us while keeping the right leg flexed. It's clear to us that we can't improve our game without practice. But it's not always so clear that we can't improve our attitude toward the game without practice, either.

8
THE WEAVE
OF LOVE

Deep in the winevault of
my love I drank, and when I came
out on this open meadow
I knew no thing at all
I lost the flock I used to drive

—John of the Cross,
The Spiritual Canticle

E go, anger, fear, impatience—to this point, we have been talking mostly about the obstacles to the true goal of golf. But everything in the universe has two aspects. Light complements dark; youth balances old age. And so, moving toward the true goal of golf consists, to paraphrase Lao-tzu, in "letting go of this and holding on to that."

Letting go of fear, anger, ego, and impatience is balanced by cultivating and holding on to a serene approach to the game. One thread of the fiber of this serenity is love—a word most of us approach with caution. Still, for the devoted golfer, it is not such a difficult word to use. What draws us so passionately to the course is a deep, abiding affection, an emotional involvement strong and steady enough to withstand the regular disappointments that are part of playing. We love the challenge of the game, the colors and shapes of the course, the feel of a sweetly struck six-iron, the flight of the ball. It's not necessary—it's probably not even wise—to spend a lot of time in the clubhouse talking about such things, but that doesn't mean we can't give them a bit more attention, inside ourselves, as we play.

Love has its own balance, its own yin-yang. There is an assertive and a receptive aspect to it; a pressing and a yielding. In any relationship the lover and the beloved most often work out an intricate arrangement of claiming and ceding or co-occupying certain territories. Preparing food, disciplining children, cleaning, earning money, managing money—in modern relationships this dance of intimacy takes millions of different forms, all seeking an optimum balance, a harmony, a peace.

Golf, too. We need to look no farther than the implements of the game in order to see the physical manifestation of this tango of force and tenderness.

Set alongside each other, the clubs in a typical bag look like they are proclaiming the whole spectrum of human emotion. There is the driver, blunt instrument if there ever was one, standing tall in the bag like a king. This is a creature of pure power, pure assertion, designed for a kind of benevolent violence. Wide, long, flat faced, the noisiest club in the bag, the driver is made not so much for moving with the course's undulations and obstacles as for transcending them by force. We speak of "ripping" a drive, or "crushing" it. And the driver, like the more forceful, active aspects of love, offers both the most joyous spectacles and the greatest opportunities for error. There is something tremendously mournful about a booming drive that screams straight off the tee and then curls right or left and deep into the woods. Like a great regret, the memory of it can haunt us, shame us, remain etched in our mind.

The fairway woods, a bit shorter and smaller, are still aligned with the driver, more closely linked to force than subtlety, more concerned with power than finesse. They are still yang energy, as the Chinese would say: connected to that part of human nature that is most active in the external world, exploring, building, bringing change.

Once we get into the long irons, however, we move a few degrees away from the realm of pure force. In golfing circles one often hears the expression: "Only God can hit the long irons." With their lengthy shafts and unforgivingly upright blades, the one-, two-, and three-irons demand a different balance of power and finesse. This might be the equivalent of the finely honed persistence that is necessary to maintain a relationship or a career across the span of decades, to love in the face of difficulty and wear, to sustain that much energy and force of will while leaving room for some delicacy. Or to exert the authority of a parent or boss without being overbearing. Hitting a three-iron properly demands a mix of sureness and touch that frightens away some golfers—which accounts for the recent popularity of seven-woods and hybrid clubs. But a well-struck long iron has a beautiful trajectory to it—a low rocket of a shot that screams away from the clubface and into the air, climbs to its apex, and then slows, seems to hover, and slips gracefully down toward the green. It is a kind of airborne graph of the well-lived life.

In the middle irons power is still involved, but it has stepped over to one side of the stage, leaving accuracy in the spotlight. Middle irons are most often the bridge between fairway and green, just as the driver is the bridge between tee and fairway. These are the clubs of the everyday aspect of love, the middle years of life, or of a long-term partnership. Not so much effort is required now; neither the glories nor the errors seem to have quite as much drama as the 270-yard drive or the mis-hit two-iron. A degree of steadiness is needed here, enough muscle to reach the green, and enough touch and wisdom to avoid the traps of middle age.

Finally there are the smaller, more delicate clubs, the short irons and wedges, and the putter. These have nothing to do with power. Everything here is touch and precision, but they have at least as much impact on the score as do the long irons and woods. "Give as much care to the end as to the beginning," Lao-tzu advised. Many golf teachers say, "Give *more* care to the end than to the beginning." The clubs from seven-iron to putter are more about considering the lay of the land, acknowledging it, yielding to it, and less about "ripping" and "crushing" and sending the ball whistling over everything at a tremendous speed. The ball moves more slowly here, the pace of the game itself slows down, etiquette comes more into play—as if we have entered the last days or minutes of a life or a love and we are required to finish gently, carefully, with a silent awareness of the other.

Part of the thrill and satisfaction of golf comes from the fact that we are using tools, an ability that is almost exclusively human. In mastering any tool we transcend the limits of our body, we claim and subdue a slightly larger piece of the surrounding mystery. The best carpenters can drive a sixteen-penny spike through the sole plate of a wall and into the bottom of a stud with a couple of smooth blows of the framing hammer. And they can also tap a four-penny nail into a strip of molding leaving no mark. And the best golfers are those who can smoothly shift gears from the forcefulness of the tee box to the subtleties of the apron of the green; who understand that if golf is about love, and love is about balance, then they need to find a flexible steadiness in themselves that is untroubled by the beasts of anger, ego, and fear—a flame that burns strong, yet flickers and bends in the wind.

108

9
Love of the Course

"It is a beautiful river," he said to his companion.

*"Yes," said the ferryman, "it is a very beautiful
river. I love it above everything. I have often listened
to it, gazed at it, and I have always learned
something from it. One can learn much from a river."*

—Hermann Hesse, *Siddhartha*

The course itself has a great deal to teach us. It serves as a metaphor for our relationship to another person, to ourselves, and to life. We can learn much from a golf course.

Worthington is, as I've mentioned, a nine-hole course, but it's a nine-hole course with a twist. The twist is that different tees are used for the "front" and "back" nines. On some holes—the third and fourth, for instance—the whites and blues are only a few yards apart and do not affect playing strategy or club selection. On other holes the tees make a moderate difference: The first plays 333 yards, then turns into a tenth that plays 351. The second goes from 322 to 347. And the ninth plays 148 and 181. On still others the whole shape of the hole is changed the second time around:

The difficult par-three fifth at 201 yards transforms itself into an easy par-four fourteenth at 240. But the moderately challenging dogleg, par-five, 476-yard eighth becomes a 406-yard, not-quite-straight, par-four seventeenth, the second hardest on the course.

And in a twist on a twist, the steep downhill sixth hole is not played the second time around. Golfers walk over to the tenth of the club's nine holes and play a flat, picturesque fifteenth, 152 to 180 yards, depending on where the tees are set on that day.

Playing any course again and again over a season or a lifetime, a golfer walks along almost every square yard of its property and comes to know it the way a farmer knows his fields, or a cobbler his knives. There is a thousand times more variety to the golfer's terrain than to the fields on which soccer, football, or baseball are played. And much more variation, too, among different courses than among, say, different hockey rinks. I've played a course with only one sand trap on it, and others where every green is surrounded by them; courses with tiny undulating greens and others where I found myself with flat, straight, thirty-yard putts; wide-open fairways, tight fairways, fairways as covered with moguls as a black-diamond ski slope; mountain courses, links courses, parkland courses, par-three courses, and courses where the shortest hole is 220 yards. This variety—and the complexity of any given layout—heightens the intimacy between player and course, an intimacy that reminds me very much of the way one person comes to know another in a friendship or marriage or a relationship between parent and child. On your home course you know it's risky to end up long and left of the seventh green—deep rough there, and an impossible downhill chip onto a steep, fast putting surface that slopes away from you. You know exactly what the prevailing wind on the fifteenth will do with your tee shot, what club to use on the eighteenth on a still, warm day. In a relationship you learn what areas of the other person's psyche to stay away from, which approaches are most satisfying and fruitful, what the weather is like on certain days, the prevailing winds, the trouble spots; you remember old battles and errors and the happy high points of the past just as, walking along the second fairway you can't help but remember the very best and worst shots you've played there over the years.

If you golf with a friend, child, parent, wife, or husband, the two worlds merge. Playing with my uncle on his home course outside Boston, I took the wrong club on the par-three fifth hole and sailed my ball over the green and into deep rough beyond the cart track. It was an awful downhill lie, and there was no way to roll the ball over the gravelly track and up the berm of the green. I made a sharp downward swing with a lob wedge and the ball flew up, popped onto the green, rolled forty feet downslope and into the hole as if it had an urgent letter to deliver there. And so there is a way now that my birdie—and my uncle's booming drive on the twelfth hole that same day—have become part of the shared experiences that constitute our relationship of nearly fifty years. In the same way that love for a child can unite two parents, love for a particular course, and for the game of golf itself, can be part of the bond of friendship.

As devoted golfers we build up a history with our course. Year upon year we see it in the sun and rain. (On winter days when I am mourning the end of the season with a particular urgency, I sometimes make the thirty-minute drive to Worthington just to look at the cold fairways. I even went out there to hit balls once or twice while there were still patches of granular snow in the shaded hollows. And I wasn't alone.) We walk it in the depths of golfing despair and the summits of golfing triumph; perhaps play thirty-six holes with an out-of-state friend we haven't seen in too long; even play a solitary round as a way of working through a career or business setback, or a deep bereavement. Over the span of a season we hit into most of the sand traps and water hazards, putt toward the hole from every conceivable angle, and—in my case at least—explore the woods and rough often enough to draw a topographical map of certain shady areas from memory.

Familiarity is said to breed contempt, but it also breeds affection. When we step up onto a first tee that we've stepped onto a thousand times before, there is a way in which it is our own history we're standing on. We have spent pieces of our allotted time on earth—wonderful hours—on this tee, on this course. How can we fail to love it?

The third hole at Worthington—the 110-degree dogleg right—is, for some reason, a particular favorite of mine. My affection for it has something to do with its beauty. You hit from a slightly elevated tee box with thick woods along the right side of the first leg, and rough along the left. The fairway rises gently and narrows as it moves toward the corner, and there is a bunker at that spot—a sort of visual trick: You must aim directly at this bunker in order to end up in the best position on the fairway. The second leg rises gently as well, with deeper rough on the left side and a stone wall and woods on the right. There is no sand or water around the green—there is something straightforward and plain about it. Yet if you miss to the right there is a steep drop-off, and if you miss to the left you will end up in three-inch rough with a downhill lie. The green itself is sloped slightly back to front and left to right, with all sorts of hidden twists in it.

It is the fourth (first time around) and fifth (second time around) hardest hole on the eighteen-hole card. I usually try to fade a wood off the tee, and then hit anywhere from a seven-iron to a three-wood to reach the green, depending upon how accurately I've placed my first shot. But the wind at Worthington is a mountain wind, fickle and strong, and it makes this a different hole every day you play it, a layout on which you can use every club in the course of a summer—a driver from the back tees on a windy day, a lob wedge from below the green to the right. I've hit my tee shot into the trees at the corner, put it in the trap there, pulled it onto the hillside— which leaves a 220-yard second shot from the rough and a downhill lie—and curled it neatly around the corner into the middle of the fairway. I once birdied it in the month of March, playing by myself on a cool, empty course with pockets of snow still lying in shaded areas of the next fairway over. And I've played with one or two members who are confident enough in their drivers to fly their tee shots over the trees at the corner, leaving themselves a 110-yard wedge to the green.

Through all of this I've formed a special affection for the third hole, and I almost always play it, well or poorly, with a calm appreciation. We have a history.

This kind of history, good and bad, is the material of which our love of the game is fashioned. Without always being aware of it, we bring it onto the course with us every time we play, just as we bring all our history with us every time we meet our father for lunch or drive our daughter home from school. Sometimes—in the middle of a bad round especially—it can be helpful to lift ourselves out of the funk of our own exasperation, look around at the course and widen the moment to include other, better moments.

You're walking down the fourteenth fairway at Worthington, overanxious and frustrated because it's such an easy par four and, instead of hitting a nice straight tee shot onto the apron of the green—something you know you're capable of doing, something you have, in fact, done—you went and lifted your drive up into the prevailing wind with some left-to-right spin on it, and it's ended up in the ragged rough at the tree line, pin-high but fifty yards away and far below the level of the green. This is a good moment to lift up your eyes, breathe, remember the third-hole feeling, take in the stately white clubhouse on the ridge and the fairways falling off to your right, remember the time you saw two fox cubs wrestling and scampering right there, twenty yards from the tee; remember the true goal of golf.

10
Nature's Steady Pulse

How many times it thundered before Franklin took the hint! How many apples fell on Newton's head before he took the hint! Nature is always hinting at us. It hints over and over again. And suddenly we take the hint.

—Robert Frost, *Comment*

Nature plays a role in our love of the game as well. Most of us spend all of our working lives and much of our recreational time indoors, and this can suffocate a primal part of us. Even the worst day of golf gets us outside.

Indoors, the immediate environment is so controllable that we find ourselves moving the air-conditioner or heating dial and changing the temperature against our skin by only a degree or two. Normal enough. But there is a way in which not being able to control the environment makes us more aware of it, and of the functioning of our own bodies. Golf exposes us to weather we would ordinarily shy away from—the heat and humidity of an August afternoon, the sharp cold of an October morning—and there is a particular joy to be taken from that, an aliveness that compensates for the discomfort and connects us again to our primitive side. And on a perfect summer morning or autumn afternoon the golf course sings to us that there is no other place to be; no better moment to ask for.

Worthington is located in one of the wildest and least-crowded parts of Massachusetts, in hilly, thickly wooded terrain where it is common to see black bear, coyotes, wild turkey, hawks, owls, and even, some people claim, mountain lions. On a summer afternoon I was walking back and forth near the edge of the trees on the par-five seventh hole, looking for my errant tee shot, when I heard a pattering of footsteps at my back, between me and the fairway. Too quick and light to be human, different rhythm than a running dog. I glanced over my shoulder and saw an adult red fox loping past in the direction of the tee. He passed within fifteen feet of me, a greeting from a different dimension of existence. Later in the year, playing alone, I climbed up to the seventeenth tee box and came upon a juvenile bald eagle there, standing placidly and nobly, startlingly large, as if watching an invisible member of her foursome address the ball. I stopped, we regarded each other for a moment, then she flew off casually into the trees on the other side of the fairway.

And last fall, on the back nine at the Mount Anthony Country Club in Bennington, Vermont, I saw a mink scampering along the edge of a waterhole, brown and sleek and alert. Hawks in New Hampshire, alligators and herons in North Carolina, water snakes in eastern Massachusetts, black swans outside Rome, frogs and geese and fish on more suburban links; the ferns, laurels, mottled shadows, and beautiful variety of a New England hardwood forest with its leaning white birches, the skin-smooth gray bark of its beech trees, the maples' spectacular display in September and October—golf courses can be little oases of natural beauty in the domesticated territory of our lives. And if we let it, nature always tugs us out of our immediate concerns, opening us out into the pastures of our larger selves, the first step in the journey of love.

It is, of course, a bit of a stretch to call golf courses natural. I'm sure they were natural in golf's earliest days, when sheep kept the fairway grass trimmed and the idea of artificially fertilized, aerated, and closely mown greens was still a century or two in the future. I've heard there are still some courses in the British Isles that retain this rough, ancient feel. But today's newer golf courses are obviously manmade, closer to a garden than a pasture, having more in common with a city park than the land of the roaming buffalo or grazing sheep. I haven't yet played a true desert course. The pictures are gorgeous—tongues of bright green on the sandy wasteland—but I suspect the unnaturalness of them would detract a bit from the pleasure. I played a few rounds recently on some fine courses on the hilly terrain outside Rome, where, as is the case in New England, the topography was eons in the making. Peculiar as it felt to hit a five-iron within spitting distance of a Roman aqueduct and, once, to shank an eight-iron into the remains of an Etruscan tomb, I felt a closer bond with nature there than I do on just-built, heavily irrigated courses.

Still, it may be the case that gardens—and golf links— soothe our spirits not in spite of the fact that they are mown, trimmed, watered, and fertilized, but because of it. We are humans, after all. We like to see the print of our own hand on things—the aqueducts, the Pyramids, the neat line of carrots in our gardens, and the neat edge of the apron of a green. Often that feeling is carried to its perverse extreme, and our hand spoils the purity and beauty of what it touches: Surely there is some work to be done toward moving golf courses into greater harmony with the natural world.

But gardens, golf links, and children are the meeting place of man's work and God's. It is right and good and natural that we love them.

11

THE MEDICINE OF OPEN SPACE

O space boundless!

—Walt Whitman, "Chants Democratic"

Zen temples have an orderly spaciousness to them that is meant to encourage and replicate the uncluttered mind. For some of us, golf courses serve the same function.

One of the side effects of living in an era that is richer and more comfortable than any in human history is that our lives are filled with a sort of visual litter. Folders, letters, advertising flyers, microwaves, cell phones, computers in all sizes, beepers, fax machines, our kids' toys, our closets full of clothes, our gizmos and bursting medicine cabinets and boxes of memorabilia—the rooms we inhabit are cluttered with things just as the modern mind is cluttered with thoughts about the state of the environment, plans for vacation, our daughter's wedding, our retirement, worries about health, money, friends, the poor and the hungry and the politically oppressed, our weekly list of errands, long as a two-iron.

Stepping across the threshold into a zendo, we shed some of the weight of this clutter and experience an immediate sense of inner relaxation. And the same is true when we step onto a golf course. Some contemporary spiritual teachers use the word *spaciousness* to describe the meditative state. It is inner spaciousness they are talking about, a soothing emptiness that wells up between the thoughts of experienced meditators, but its importance applies to the exterior world as well. The fairway offers us the same avenue into interior calm that is offered by the sight of the ocean, or the desert, or a pasture covered with snow. Look, it says, pause here a minute, take a load off.

This idea of emptiness or spaciousness lies at the heart of descriptions of interior peace in almost every tradition. Christians are more likely to describe it as "love" or "the presence of God" or "the loving presence of God," but secular and religious contemplatives alike talk about a quieting of the mind—some kind of inner tidiness and openness—as being a prerequisite to love, to happiness. It is interesting to note that almost all very good golfers use the same language when describing their mental situation during the golf swing: a thought-free, focused, positive presence.

But something in the human animal is afraid of this quiet, empty place. We rush to fill our interior spaces with noise and busyness. I know that when I hit a poor golf shot, my instinct is to hurry after the ball and rectify matters as quickly as possible. A second troublesome shot and my mind goes scurrying around for answers—remember to flatten the swing plane, to hit down, to shift the left hip out of the way. Every golfer has known the experience of having a bad shot or a bad hole change the entire tone of the rest of the round—like a dark curtain being let down over the day. The worse we play the more we think, and the more we think the worse we play.

It goes without saying that thinking and figuring have their place—it's a good thing to know what we've done wrong if the ball goes off target—but all the great players insist that, once we are in a match, the most important thing is to close down the mind and simply trust. Same as what the mystics all say. But how difficult it is to give up the safety blanket of obsessive mental scrambling and just swing, or just be. How much training and practice it requires, how much interior work. How much courage, too, because without that blanket the world can appear fearfully empty and cold, silent as the dark reaches of space.

There is something splendid about that emptiness, though. You feel it on the first tee early in the morning, or walking alone along a fairway near dusk, just as you feel it at the ocean or in a quiet stretch of meditation. *Emptiness* is not really the right word for it. The right word, if it could be found, would include the quality of emptiness, but the emptiness would echo with a single clear note. There would be, behind the note, camouflaged by it but palpable, the essence of sound and color and touch, a hint of some awesome spark in the cells, the tremble of life. Golfers would recognize it immediately, because the game they love is composed of small moments, one-second bursts of activity amid a great airy expanse of nothing. The wideness, the openness of the fairway, and then this ball you can hide in a child's hand. I will not risk saying it aloud, but I sometimes have the thought that golf is divine poetry, the Creator's metaphor for what he has made: the unfathomable enormity of all space, and within it this hard spinning sphere upon which so much seems to rest; the illusion of movement and completion—tee to green—that only brings us back, perhaps scarred and wiser, to the beginning. I will not risk it. Golf is just a game. Golf is just a game. The open course is just the field of our mind on which that great and terrible game is played.

12
The Senses: Gateways to Love

How good is man's life, the mere living! how fit to employ
All the heart and the soul, and the senses forever in joy.

—Robert Browning, "Saul"

I once did some carpentry work for an elderly man on Martha's Vineyard who was full of theories about things. He was a kindly, affable fellow, and while I was nailing together new flower boxes for his garden he talked to me about birds, plants, wildlife, his girlfriend, the various facets of his philosophy. The notion of his that most impressed me was the idea that religious services, of whatever faith, are designed to reach the soul through all five senses. Walk into a church, temple, mosque, or shrine and there is usually some kind of visual stimulus: stained-glass windows, a crucifix, a statue of the Buddha; the great arches, columns, and elaborate altars of the famous European cathedrals; the perfect austerity of a Zen hall or the colorful complexity of Tibetan Buddhism's mandalas; the many gods and goddesses of Hinduism, the sacred symbols of Judaism, the sea-blue tiles in the mosques of Central Asia.

There are songs, hymns, and bells for the ear; incense and flowers and candles for the nose; a communion wafer, or blessed foods, or ritual meals for the tongue. And every religion makes some use of the sense of touch, even if it is nothing more than the holding of two hands together in a posture of prayer or meditation.

This man's theory was that the senses are the pathways to our innermost self, our essence, our soul—and God or the Great Spirit or the Divine Intelligence or the Nameless One makes use of all of them to convey His or Her or Its message.

This is applicable to more earthly love as well. Parent to child, husband to wife, friend to friend—love moves along the channels of touch, sight, sound, and, where there's cooking involved, smell and taste.

With the possible exception of taste (though some people chew on tees or pencils), the senses are all brought into use during a game of golf, too. The smartest golfers pay attention to the way the sand feels beneath their shoes—loose and dry, wet, coarse, hard packed—because this information will affect their bunker shot: how much they open the blade, how far they hit behind the ball, how much roll they will allow for once it is on the green. They use their feet, and sometimes hands, to get a sense of the firmness or sponginess of the green, which will determine the speed at which they want to hit the ball, which will in turn determine the amount of break they allow for. They take their glove off to better feel the grip of the putter, and they learn to sense the weight of the clubhead as they swing. To amateurs and nonplayers, a professional golfer's obsession with fine-tuning his equipment can seem as contrived as the vocabulary of wine tasting to a drinker of five-dollar rosé. But tour pros bore holes in the meaty part of their wedges, or add half an inch to the shaft of their driver, or a few ounces of electrical tape to their nine-iron not out of some urge to show off, but because their sense of touch has been refined to the point where they notice things other players miss. Whether it is the club or the course or their hands, they have trained themselves to pay heightened attention to the physical world, to sharpen the senses.

Their love for and understanding of the game is that subtle, but there are plenty of high handicappers who love golf as much as, if not more than, people who get paid to play it. They, too, love the feel of the club in their hands or their feet on the fairway, or just the sensation of the breeze against bare forearms. Before the introduction of spikeless cleats we used to love the tapping of metal spikes on a tar parking lot. We love the sound of the shaft cutting through air, the click of a well-hit iron shot, the gentle slapping sound a ball makes when it hits against the surface of the green after a high, arcing flight, the sight of the different shades of green along a fairway, its undulations and shadows, the neat cut of the apron around a putting surface. Surely every golfer loves to hear the sound of a ball rattling into the bottom of the cup.

One way to bring the mind into the present—in the meditation hall and on the links—is to pay attention to the subtler information our ears are receiving: the sputter of a golf cart engine two fairways over; the cries of gulls or the singing of frogs if we are near water, crickets if we are near the end of the day, and the raucous families of crows that live in the trees if we are walking along the seventh fairway at Worthington. Quite often we don't hear the intricate symphony going on every instant around us, because we are, as the saying goes, "lost in thought." The inner workings of the mind—worries, plans, hopes, angers—have overwhelmed its more basic functions, cut us off from our own sense of being alive, cast us out of the moment and into the past or future. It's a nice little exercise to try on the course—especially as we're walking from shot to shot, especially if we're wound up about our game that day: Just listen for a few seconds. Or simply take in the contours of the fairway or the color of the sky or the trajectory of our playing partner's shot; or smell the mown grass, or taste the fertilizer on that tee or the paint on that pencil.

Perhaps all this sounds a bit too soft edged and saccharine, but it's not about dreaminess and sleepy smiles. Just the opposite, in fact: It's about not sacrificing what is real for the sake of our own sweet or miserable musings. It's about having ears and hearing.

Thoreau, Whitman, D. T. Suzuki, Teresa of Avila, Buddha, Jesus, Black Hawk, Emily Dickinson, Einstein, Merton, Hazrat Khan, Martin Buber, Gandhi, Baldwin, Monet—all the mystics, most of the artists and lovers, anyone with much of value to say about the human predicament has offered a piece of advice that crosses every religious, racial, political, and gender boundary: Pay attention. Golf, with its slow pace and abundant silences, its need to eliminate distractions, its symphony of sensory input, offers the perfect opportunity for letting the senses open into the present. Golf is something we work at, but mainly it's something we *play*. There aren't many opportunities for play in the adult life, whereas for children it is their profession, their reason for being. Watching a child play, you see a creature who is fully attentive, completely immersed in the sound and feel and smell and sight of being; completely and joyously buried in the present. As the mystics are fond of repeating: That present is the threshold to the room of real love.

13

BEAUTY: LOVE'S PARTNER

A thing of beauty is a joy forever.
Its loveliness increases; it will never
Pass into nothingness; but still will keep
A bower quiet for us, and a sleep
Full of sweet dreams, and health, and quiet breathing.

—Keats, "Endymion"

Beauty is another way in which golf and love are linked, and another aspect of our attraction to the game. With its different species of trees and flowering bushes, its various types and colors of sand, shapes of bunkers and water hazards, and lengths, shades, and species of grass, a golf course is a kind of living sculpture, a salve for the modern eye. Older courses display the irregularities of the terrain they were cut from, and many of them are pleasing in a natural and effortless way. With the increased popularity of golf has come an increase in demand for new, longer, more challenging courses, and former tour champions—Tom Weiskopf, Gary Player, Raymond Floyd, and Jack Nicklaus to name a few—have joined famous old architects like Robert Trent Jones, and famous new ones like

Pete Dye, in putting their distinctive mark on eighteen-hole layouts.

The architect's goal is to push and prod golfers toward the edges of their ability. Length and shape of holes, placement of trees, bunkers, and water hazards, slope and contour of the greens, moguls in the fairway—architects use these and other variables in a thousand combinations to humble the long hitter or frighten the timid putter, or to reward accuracy or power or the willingness to take risks. At the same time, they create something of real visual complexity and beauty, and do what artists always do: urge us to pay closer attention to the world.

The more we make ourselves small and quiet in the Taoist sense, empty in the Zen sense, interiorly still in the way of Thoreau and Teresa of Avila, the more the beauty of our surroundings leaps out at us and quiets the mind still further. The smaller the ego, the more powerfully we are able to love, and the easier it is to appreciate beauty. And then the beautiful object or beautiful aspect of a person feeds love and strengthens the fiber of our quiet that much more. Many of the mystics speak of "ecstasies," and I wonder if this isn't what fuels that joy: this cycle of smallness, attentiveness, and appreciation—which then makes us smaller, which makes us more attentive, which makes us more appreciative.

Ecstasy may be too strong a word for what we feel on the golf course, but then again golf has such a powerfully addictive quality that it must strike a very sweet spot at a very deep level. Part of this sweetness comes from the beauty of the field on which the game is played. Not long ago I watched Jack Nicklaus on TV, walking up the fairway in the Pebble Beach Pro-Am. He had just hit a mediocre tee shot, but he was striding along with his head up and a wonderful, happy expression on his face. *Happy* is not strong enough a word for it; you could almost say he was ecstatic. It obviously wasn't the tee shot he was ecstatic about. When the camera angle changed, you could see that he was looking at a beautifully kept fairway and green at the edge of the Pacific.

We don't have to play Pebble Beach, special as it is, to experience those kinds of moments. The smoothness and

147

shading of any green, the rolling and tilting of any fairway, even the cut and color of a sand trap on a plain public course can lift us out of ourselves.

Plato said: "Beholding beauty with the eye of the mind, he will be enabled to bring forth, not images of beauty but reality (for he has hold not of an image but of a reality) and bringing forth and nourishing true virtue to become the friend of God and be immortal, if mortal man may."

For many avid golfers, the beauty of the course serves as a sort of regular mind-rinse. There is a fair amount of ugliness in modern life—plain apartment houses, garish gas stations, cheap plastic furniture. It accumulates in the inward eye, in the memory, like so much oily newspaper in the corners of a tar alley. The inward cleansing golf provides is an important part of our love of the game. Weekly or twice weekly or, for the most fortunate among us, daily, we can stroll along an unfenced emerald fastasyscape, a kind of Eden for the eye.

It is no accident that throughout human history the greatest designers, stonemasons, and artists have been at-

148

tracted to creating spaces of worship; no accident that monasteries—those workshops of the inner world—have been set in places of great natural beauty. The view from the monastery grounds moves its contemplative inhabitants, inspires them, cleans them out. Which is just what happens to the golfer on the course. Which is why those of us in the colder climates suffer from all sorts of wintertime neuroses and withdrawal symptoms: For so much of the year, our place of prayer is inaccessible.

14
THE RELIGION
OF GOLF

Religion in its humility restores man to his only dignity, the courage to live by grace.

—George Santayana,
"Dialogues in Limbo"

For the serious player, golf is a type of religion. This is another troublesome word, because at one end of the spectrum there are those who cherish their faith so much they don't want it compared to more secular pursuits; and at the other end are those who had such a terrible time with the religion of their youth, or see it only as the cause of wars and divisiveness, that they will close the book on that word in an instant. By calling golf a religion, I do not mean it replaces the worship of Christ, Yahweh, Mohammed, Krishna, Buddha, or any other figure of our devotion. I don't mean it in the narrowly used sense of the word at all. The regular practice of any religion is designed to pull us free—for a few minutes or a few hours—from our mundane concerns, those ordinary pleasures and duties, work and worry, in which it is so easy to bury ourselves. Buried there, we lose sight of the larger picture and take refuge in busyness, clutter, and chatter. Religion is supposed to give us some perspective on that. Ancient rituals like fasting and the repetition of phrases or gestures were developed in order to break the inertia of the everyday mind; to knock us out of the habitual patterns of thought and behavior. To snap us free from what sages of all religions insist is a sort of hypnosis, an illusory sense of how things actually are.

Golf can do this, too. We have our Scriptures—the book of rules; our commentaries—in the form of golf books and golf magazines. We have, in the course itself, a temple of worship to which we wear certain types of clothing, and which we keep neatly maintained. We have the course pro, a sort of priest or mullah, who acts as an intermediary between us and the higher power: he teaches, offers counsel and sympathy, and organizes the weekend services we call tournaments. Most courses have the equivalent of monks or nuns, those men and women who seem to give up sex, a home life, and a regular job to accumulate blessings in the afterlife by their near-constant presence at the place of worship. There is something soothing about driving up to the clubhouse and seeing these people in their usual spot, performing a function that we would perform, too, if we weren't so carried away by the cares and temptations of the worldly life.

We tithe to our place of worship either each time we visit or in one lump sum at the start of the year. We have our rituals, our silences, even, as some other religions do, administrative hierarchies—the PGA and USGA—that canonize and penalize and amass money and determine the dates of the high holidays at our meccas: Augusta, Pebble Beach, Pinehurst.

Sometimes golf doesn't perform this function of lifting us free from more worldly matters. Sometimes it gets incorporated into the busyness and turns into just another fading pleasure at which we grasp and over which we whirl and worry.

For most people, though—even the most frantic and least-peaceful players—there are sublime moments on the course, mini enlightenments. These might come after a great shot or a thrilling victory, but they might also descend upon us for no apparent reason as we walk along the eleventh fairway in a light wind, stand on the first tee at dawn, or drive our cart up the little rise near the eighteenth green when the sun is about to set, the flagstick casts a long shadow, and the windows of the clubhouse glow in the dusk. These moments are golf's little gifts to us. *They* are what keep us coming back.

The real value of them, perhaps the real value of golf, lies in the vision they afford us of our best selves, our capacity for peace. If we have a wonderful day on the course—either because we've played well, enjoyed the company of friends, or appreciated the beauty of the game—a sort of time-release capsule of happiness is implanted in us. Echoes of the joy of those hours resound in the rest of our lives—for an hour, a day, a week. In this way the pleasure golf affords can be compared to a quiet stretch of meditation, to lovemaking, to a revealing hour in the therapist's office or in church, to the transcendent moments between a parent and child, or between two old friends when a blossom of pure affection appears after a stretch of bad weather.

Life cannot be composed only of moments like those, any more than a round of golf can be composed only of perfect shots, or a career or a marriage can be composed purely of successes and compounded joys. Illness, death, depression, failure, estrangement—those things are as persistent and unavoidable as the bad golf shots that find their way into the rounds of even the greatest players.

No amount of advice, practice, or devotion is going to eliminate those shots completely. And even the most perfect swings start to deteriorate with age: Scores swell, distances shrink. This is the source of real sadness for most of us, because an essential aspect of our love of the game is the hope of improvement. I know that golf would lose some of its appeal for me if I didn't imagine myself playing better, or at least smarter. But the sorrow we feel over losing our ability as we age is probably the best argument for cultivating our innermost game, that part of our love that does not depend on the length of our drives or the sweet trajectory of our five-irons. If looked at through the lens of the mystics, the fullness of our passion for golf cannot be siphoned away by aging. If we're wise enough or lucky enough to dilute the sticky ego, to step away from our anger and frustration and play through our subtle fears, then those little glimpses of enlightenment that we feel on the course can be expanded and carried over into our nongolfing life—so much more important an arena. We can begin to inhabit a quieter interior world, less vulnerable to the winds of fate. The real "zone" we want to find and reside in is a sort of fully engaged detachment—not so detached that we don't try or care, and yet not so engaged that good shots and poor shots, good and bad fortune, even the end of our golfing days knock us up and down like puppets on twitching strings.

The detached joy of the enlightened golfer is a place that is focused and quiet and real, the place the mystics, whatever their differences, all speak from, the place all religions and well-lived lives point toward. As we travel in the direction of this place our handicap will probably come down. How sweet that would be. Still, a lower handicap is not what makes us love the game as madly as we do. And it's not the true purpose of golf.